BREAKING THE CYCLE
From Special Ed. to Ph.D

Dr. Eboni Wilson

BREAKING THE CYCLE
Copyright © 2003 by Dr. Eboni Wilson

Published by
In Time Publishing & Media Group
75 East Wacker Drive, 10th Floor
Chicago, Illinois 60601
www.intimepublishing.com

ISBN# 0-9746384-0-4

Dedication

This book is dedicated to my late brother Bernard Bennie Wilson. Unfortunately he was another statistic of inner city violence. May he rest in peace. This book is also dedicated to the young, innocent kids in the ghetto who, unfortunately, continue living blind and in poverty. I wrote this book for those who are suffering as I once did, and for those who need to know what goes on in the world of a ghetto child.

CONTENTS

CONTENTS (CONT'D)

ACKNOWLEDGEMENT

I first want to thank the God who created us all; the God who is the good in everyone; the God who lacks the feeling of hate in his heart; God who looks at life as precious no matter what a person's skin color is; the God who gave me the vision and the understanding of how our world works; the God who gave me the tenacity to change the miserable conditions that these innocent kids live through every day; the God of love.

I want to acknowledge those who have helped me on my path to where I am today. I would like to thank my high school coach who helped "put me on the market" for college scouts to recognize my gift. Coach Johnson also helped me see another side of life—how it operates, and the rules for functioning within it. I also want to thank Coach Shapell for helping me see how mainstream society functions. I want to thank him for opening up the weight room for me every day at six o'clock in the morning; I needed that release before my day began. I want to thank Jon Douglas for giving me a job outside of my community. He helped me understand that there is another life outside of the 'hood. Although he did not know it at the time, he changed the way I viewed my society and life in general. He helped my ambitions grow into something other than what I saw daily.

Dear Children,

I wish to acknowledge you, the thousands and thousands of innocent ghetto kids suffering everyday from a life you do not deserve to live. I want you to know that I understand your sufferings; I have been where you are today. I want you to know that I wrote this book for you. I wanted everyone to hear your cries and to understand the pain you face. I wanted you, the ghetto youth, to understand that you are trained to become what you see everyday. You are trained to be thugs. You are designed to accept what you were born into, and at the same time, you are being persuaded to think that this is the right way to live. The people in your life all play a role in how you view it: your friends, your environment, the adults in your life, the media, and even your own thought process. Your society is designed to keep you in the dark.

The life you are living right now is not the life you have to live forever. The anger you feel in your heart is not the anger you are supposed to feel for the rest of your life. You are programmed to think this way; you are influenced to believe your skin is a sin. You are trained to look at each other as if you were without value, so you talk to each other with disrespect, you kill each other out of ignorance, and give up on life because you are taught not to be persistent. We, who live in the ghetto. are taught to embrace its mentality. What is the ghetto mentality? It is a mentality that does not define you as a person, but a mentality that defines your position in life.

My ghetto children, you are programmed to say, "F--- life." You are programmed since birth to believe that ghetto kids don't need education because they won't live long enough to use it. Although you don't realize it now, every interaction you have in life, whether it's positive or negative, stays in your brain and in your thought process forever. When you hear people talk about killing, you become numb to it. You don't look at it as a big deal. When you see people who look like you selling dope, you become numb to it. When those around you don't embrace school and knowledge, you begin subconsciously to fall into the norm as well, believing that it's not a big deal. And before you know it, your life has slipped away and you begin to fall into the ghetto norm. You feel that this is your life and that you must simply deal with it.

I am here to let you know that the information that has been fed to you since birth is a lie. Don't believe it. Trust me, I know. You can become a doctor, a lawyer, a teacher, a scientist—anything you desire. You have a brain just like any other human being in the world; how you use it determines your individuality.

You are not destined to fail; you are destined to prevail. You are not destined to be a thug; you are destined to grow and blossom so that you can show love to your child. You are not destined to live a short life, but you are destined to gain knowledge and overcome the miserable conditions you were dealt at first light.

I want to acknowledge you, the ghetto seed—the seed that is not being nurtured and constantly bleeds. I want to shine the light on you, the beautiful child who can see it through. I want to water you with love, so that you grow and blossom from below. You and I together, we all can be free. Not free in the physical sense, but free within our minds, because through them, the purest light can shine.

FROM SPECIAL ED. TO PH.D
The liberation process of man named Eboni

From the pits of the ghetto,
to the land that's mellow
I rose

Through the hunger and pain.
I found a way to gain
I rose

From begging for money, because my
mother wouldn't put food in my tummy
I rose

From pumping gas to get some
hard earned cash
I rose

I fought through the adversity,
and refuse to submit with mercy
I rose

From the confinement of the ghetto's gate,
I emerged away from the hate
I rose

From losing a brother, and having a
crack head for a mother
I rose

From having a burden of a crack
addicted father, a man who never really
seemed to bother
I rose

I battled, and won the war of poverty,
I defied the odds on my society
I rose

From sole-less shoes, and inner-city blues
I rose

I refused to submit to the lies and deceit,
because I recognized the trap that was
designed for me
I rose

From the crack cocaine that destroyed
my family, that powerful substance,
that kills you rapidly
I rose

From my grave, I recognized the façade,
and chose a new path to pave
I rose

I journeyed to that distant place,
unaware of my fate, yet overwhelmed
with joy, cause I now can liberate
I rose

From the stereotype that was placed on
me, the illusion that I could clearly see,
because I yearned to be free
I rose

I've reached the place that many would
cherish, I shocked those who thought
my dreams would parish
I rose

It took me 24 years to finally get here,
now I can breathe because I no longer
have to lie in fear
I rose

I wrote this book with the intention of opening the minds of individuals across the nation. Some think that it is impossible to dilute the gangs, drugs, and violence of the inner city. Others think that the ills of the ghetto community cannot be rectified, and that it is a fairytale to believe such leaps can be made. Such a vision of a productive society seems blurry to most of the residents of this poverty-stricken environment. Yet there was a time when no one could imagine that the world was round, and look how wrong they were. Ideas that seemed far-fetched and unrealistic 100 years ago, exist today; such unimaginable innovations like television, computers, the Internet, and even integration.

I wish for those who read my story, along with my poetry, to gain an understanding that life is precious—an understanding that a society of people should not have to live in such dire conditions that they are convinced their lives serve no worth. My poetry captures the struggles of inner-city youth in an artistic format. Written all throughout my childhood, I relate to different experiences I felt and the feelings I needed to express at the moment. I was one of these children. These innocent children lack a positive vision. With a positive vision of self and life, they can dilute the cycle of the ghetto. In time, I will show those who doubt, that your mind can be nurtured into something that will allow you to flourish into a positive form. In time, the light will appear to all of you who have been living in the dark.

This book takes you on a journey through the life of Eboni Kentay Wilson: the ups, downs, trials, and tribulations of growing up in the ghetto of South Central Los Angeles. Not only will I take you on a journey through where I was, but also to where I have arrived. I am a man that has a vision of a better life for inner-city children, and I hope to open your third eye. Your third eye is what has been covered from the realities and misfortunes that exist in the life of kids growing up in the ghetto. The eye allows you to see beyond the obvious and into the hearts of a suffering people.

STRUGGLING

When your entire family live in the ghetto, from your cousin tear, to your aunt may
YOU KNOW YOU'RE STRUGGLING.
When the light bill is in your name, the gas in your brother's, and the bill collectors are after your mother,
YOU KNOW YOU'RE STRUGGLING.
When the cops are on your back cause your mama smoke crack, You know you struggling.
When you're so broke you have to cash food stamps for some soap,
YOU KNOW YOU'RE STRUGGLING.
When you have to cash in cans to get some pro-wing style vans,
YOU KNOW YOU'RE STRUGGLING.
When you have to fight to stay off your knees, get up early in the morning to help folks with their groceries,
YOU KNOW YOU'RE STRUGGLING.
When times get too rough and you have to go out and beg cause you don't have enough,
YOU KNOW YOU'RE STRUGGLING.
When your hunger turns to anger and your anger turns to hate, you stop caring and welcome all fate,
YOU KNOW YOU'RE STRUGGLING.
When your ignorance gets the best of you, with survival as your guide, you stop begging and Pleading and welcome savage ways to survive,
YOU KNOW YOU'RE STRUGGLING.

Chapter One

MY DYSFUNCTIONAL FAMILY

My mother had four boys; I am the second to the youngest. My parents separated when I was three-years-old, and I, like many children in the ghetto grew up deprived of a father figure. Now being a man, I wonder how a "father" would have influenced my life. Only when we become adults can we look back in retrospect, without anger, and without resentment, and wonder what could have been. I barely had any special moments with a father who other boys related to: no late night chats, no feeling of protection, and no one picking me up off the ground when I scrapped my knee. I don't have very many memories of a father, and even fewer of a daddy. Rather, I have memories, few and far between, of a man named Benny.

Benny, my father, was tall—about 6'2" and my first memory of Benny occurred when I was three-years-old and a firecracker exploded in my hand. I can remember him coming outside and asking, "What did you do?" Then he whipped me and sent me to my room. The idea of living in a home with both parents is a foreign concept to me. I was too young to remember a time that I lived with my mother and father under the same roof and looking back at the people they were, maybe that was a good thing.

My parents did not get along at all! When they spent any

time at all together, my mother cursed at my father. Their fights replay in my head as if it were only yesterday.

"That no-good bastard! He better stay the f--- away from my kids and me!" or, "I hate that son-of-a-b----!" Profanity was no stranger in our household and my mother never held back her feelings for our sake. She would rather everyone in the neighborhood knew her feelings on any given subject, than keep her thoughts to herself; everyone always knew what she thought, whether they wanted to or not.

Needless to say, we had a less than traditional family. Each member of my family did his own thing. We all had to fend for ourselves, and if we happened to do something together, it was only by coincidence. We rarely celebrated special events like holidays, awards, or achievements together. When people talk about their memories of Christmas mornings, birthdays, or special events, I have nothing to contribute. I don't long to be with my family during holiday seasons, or wonder where we are all going to get together for Thanksgiving. We might have lived under the same roof (at times anyway), but we lived very separate lives and had very separate agendas.

Neither of my parents graduated from high school, and both worked on and off at minimum wage jobs. I never knew what type of work my father did because he was rarely around, and my mother never talked about him. When he did come home it was only for a short time, and that infuriated my mother. She felt he wasn't doing his part in raising us, and she had to pick up the slack.

As a child, I never understood why my father stayed away as much as he did. It was so typical in that ghetto environment that I never gave it a second thought. In my eyes, he did what he had to do in life, and I did what I had to do. Now I realize that he liked his freedom, and he thought we took that freedom away from him. There are many different types of men in this world— not better or worse, but different. The trick is deciding what kind of man you want to be before responsibility arises; and then being that man no matter the weight on your shoulders or how much of a challenge it is.

❧

Now I think that my father regrets what kind of man he was. He stayed away from his children because he wanted to avoid my mother, grandmother, and all the drama that existed at our house; but he didn't realize the repercussions of sacrificing his children for his precious freedom. In retrospect, the cost of his selfishness was nearly insurmountable. I once heard Maya Angelou say, "We do the best that we can with what we know, and when we know more, we will do better." Now I think that Benny knows more than he did then, and he has tried to do better, but there are some moments in time that are lost forever.

My father was a mellow person. He didn't like a lot of drama in his life, but my mother was the complete opposite! Her very existence is defined by the drama that she was involved in on any given day. She is what I like to refer to as a "drama queen." My father did not waste his time with frivolous antics, unlike my mother who liked to make a scene in front of anyone and everyone who was willing to watch her show. I think her drama contributed to my father's absence in our lives. He left someone who lived to embarrass him, who could blame him?

My father is a lady's man and always lived with other women who took care of him. I don't know of a time when my father lived alone.

My mother was a self-serving woman who liked to get her way. She used guilt and pity as her weapons of choice. She preyed on people's sympathies and constantly tried to get those around her to feel sorry for her, ultimately helping her get whatever it was she wanted. I didn't fall for her smoke and mirrors act as a child, nor do I fall for it as an adult, and that has caused tension in our relationship. Rather then give-in to her pestering, I played along with her until she got tired of trying to con me for my money, my time, and my sympathy.

My mother was a single parent that had to bear the weight of raising her four kids alone. She was someone you didn't not want to mess with. Even though she was short and heavyset, my brothers and I always feared her wrath. Being a single mother with four boys, she knew that she had to hold her ground—often she went to the extreme. My mother made sure that we never did or said anything to refute what she felt was right. On any given day, she would wake up in the morning and if the house was not clean, she would kick our butts without asking a single question. She whipped us by anything and everything she could get her hands on: a belt, an extension cord, a switch, and even the phone cord. She never missed an opportunity to chastise us, while taking her frustrations out on her children because she couldn't vent to anyone else.

Without a steady man in the house, she felt lonely and she had numerous flings with boyfriends who were in and out of our home. They ranged from ex-cons to big-time drug dealers, and my brothers and I saw them all. Meanwhile, the relationship she had with my father continued to grow distant and strained. They rarely spoke to each other, and when he would come over to see us, they would argue the entire time about how much they didn't like each other. All the pettiness between them limited the amount of time my brothers and I saw our father even more, .

She depended on my grandmother and a welfare check to help her take care of her children. When I was five, she couldn't find a job and she felt minimum wage jobs were a waste because the government was meeting her needs. You have to understand that my mother likes to get whatever she can get for free. She loves scamming people, including her own children.

When I graduated with my bachelor's degree, my mother came to Washington to attend my graduation. While she was visiting, she managed to steal my graduation cloth, pictures of my brother who has passed away, certificates, awards, and any other valuables that she could get her hands on. I wouldn't have cared as much if she had just stolen my clothing or material possessions. She took things that had sentimental value to me, things that meant something to me because they represented what I had accomplished despite her, her addiction, and her ignorance. In that moment, my childhood came full circle and my ambition was renewed because I was staring at a reminder of what I never wanted to be.

My mother was satisfied with a life in the ghetto. She had no problem living on welfare for the rest of her life. Unless, one of her children is successful, then she expects them to replace the government and support her. What she failed to realize is that it's not a child's job to support his parents; it was her job to support us as we were growing up, and she failed to do so.

She is a product of the system. I refuse to believe that the sole purpose of welfare is to aid the poor. It is a government-constructed crutch, designed to keep the poor, poor. She, like many others in the 'hood, couldn't see beyond a monthly check. My mother is another statistic of how the cycle of poverty plagues the inner-city environments of America. It's easy to hear about poverty when it's a statistic, or a study. It's a different reality when it's your people, your friends, your family, and even your own mother.

My oldest brother, Peanut, was the shortest of us all, but by far the leading product of "the system." He first went to jail around the age of fourteen for stealing cars, and from that point on, he has constantly been in and out of jail. By the age of fifteen, he was sent to a juvenile home in Canoga Park where he remained for the rest of his juvenile years. Peanut had a difficult time giving up his life of crime because he fell victim to the temptations of gangs at an early age. He was affiliated with a neighborhood gang called N.H.B., otherwise known as a blood gang, where he joined at age fifteen. He yearned for a tight knit family that only his gang offered. They offered him love, friendship, food, and money—the necessities his family couldn't provide. Eventually he became completely absorbed with the pleasures of the gang and the inner city, but who could blame him?

Growing up in the 'hood, we were surrounded by violence, gangs, and what appeared to him to be a hopeless future. People who aren't from the ghetto have a hard time understanding why we do the things we do. I want you to understand that people don't join gangs for the hell of it, but out of necessity. They join for protection, for love, and for acceptance. Many inner-city kids are forced to join gangs to find the necessities people take for granted. Now imagine facing that reality everyday as a five-year-old. It's more than a Spike Lee movie; it's a harsh reality and in that situation, it's hard to see beyond the positive things a gang has to offer.

Peanut concentrated all his energy on his gang family. He chose this life and no one could convince him that he had made the wrong choice! Besides, no one was there to tell him that he was on the wrong path. He figured he had nothing to lose and everything to gain, and he made his decision. Our community was like a prison; therefore, he figured the consequences of his actions wouldn't be worse than what he faced on a daily basis. He was lost in a society that swallowed him up in negativity and hopelessness: he gave up on himself before he ever got started. He did not care what happened to him or what he needed to do to get what he wanted—a trait he inherited from our mother.

Peanut was not born this way, but society conditioned him to adapt to his environment for survival, and he became a hard-nosed gang member who was not afraid to die. He was slowly molded to be the man he is today—a convicted felon, struggling to stay alive. He was once excited about school and earning good grades, but that form of gratification began to fade as he grew up. He used to play with other children in the neighborhood before his environment corrupted him. I am not defending his decision to join a gang, but I want you to understand why he did.

Peanut was not strong enough to go against the grain his whole life, and he gave-in to his environment. Who could blame him? He was welcomed with open arms into a society that thrived on ignorance, murder, theft, and hatred, but he was no longer alone. With these elements implanted in his mind, Peanut indulged in negative ways to survive. He became content with what the ghetto had to offer him. Unfortunately, that was a quick route to jail, and a rapid journey towards death. Peanut could not see what was on the other side of the tracks and had no frame of reference to imagine a better life. He was convinced that drugs, gangs, and hustling were all that existed in his own manifestation of American society. Before the system trapped Peanut into ignorance, hate, drugs, gangs, and poverty, he was a decent kid who had aspired to be an artist. He abandoned that dream, and accepted his fate to exist inside the ghetto, as many black men do. He became a statistic of the prison system with no real hope for making it in mainstream society. My brother fell into the trap of the 'hood with no one ther to pull him out. The trap I'm referring to is poverty and it takes the form of unemployment and welfare, thus allowing the cycle to continue by insuring that its victims are dependent on the system, rather than themselves.

My second oldest brother, Bernard, fell into the temptations of the ghetto, just as Peanut had. He was the only one of my brothers that I resembled. He joined a gang called the HollyHood Piru at age fourteen. Although once he dreamed of becoming an electrical engineer, he didn't see any real way out of his environment. For kids in the 'hood, dreaming is never the problem; it's learning how to reach those dreams that tangles us up. Peanut was never given the tools to map a path to a better future nor the opportunity to create a clear direction for his goals. He was consumed by drugs, gangs, and violence and became convinced that the only way to succeed was to start selling drugs and robbing people.

Eventually Bernard found a dream outside of violence and drugs that he felt he could accomplish; he began rapping. Only then was a constructive and creative side of him revealed.

He loved what he did and eventually was successful enough to meet with rap icon, 2Pac Shakur and talk about his future.

Bernard and Peanut had collaborated numerous times plotting different crimes they were going to commit. They didn't care what the repercussions were for their actions. Our environment nurtured violent male activities, and encouraged my brothers' behavior by enabling them to continue to commit crimes, thus hindering their ability to see past their experiences.

My younger brother, Travie, was a socialite. He was too caught up in his friends to get into trouble at a young age. He was the most spoiled of all of us and believed that he should get whatever he wanted since he was the youngest—a curse that follows him to this day. The problem with Travie being spoiled is that it allowed him to develop the mentality that people owe him something and they should cater to his needs. To this day, he still carries this trait, and it has proven to be the most detrimental to his future. Travie never grew out of that stage; he still feels that the world owes him something and that he shouldn't have had to wait so long to get it. We all know someone like this; someone we want to slap across the back of the head every time his pity party starts! Hey, there's one in every family.

Travie wasn't all bad—he was the comedian of the family. He was always searching for a laugh by doing something silly, saying something outrageous, or making a ridiculous face. His very presence just made you want to laugh. He was extremely short with chubby cheeks and a frown, and he looked nothing like me. Looking back on my childhood, I am extremely thankful that he was such a funny kid. There were times when he was the only thing that kept our household sane and lifted our spirits a little higher.

Growing up in the mid-eighties when gang violence was at an all-time high, my brothers and I were surrounded by negative influences. We'd seen it all; murders, robberies, street fights, brutal beatings, drug raids, and starvation. We faced these tragedies everyday; they were not something we could run from; we were immersed in them. We had to endure these misfortunes day in and day out. Not having food in the refrigerator or clean clothes to wear to school, our lifestyle was completely engulfed by hunger and poverty: two conditions that proved to be the roots of our family tree. We started with nothing and tried to make scraps into meals. My brothers and I had to make pancakes out of flour and water, and milk out of powder. We were the poorest of all the families in the neighborhood. We had nothing. We accepted hand-me-downs from our friends' parents who felt sorry for us. I especially remember when we would ask our neighbors for food. My mother would force us to go and ask. She was embarrassed, but didn't do anything to change our circumstances. In fact, I can remember several times when my mother did not pay the bills, and we lived in the dark because the electric company had shut off our lights. At least they have lights in prison.

There was a time when my brother Peanut went to juvenile hall because he stole a car, and I can remember feeling, it's safer for him to be in jail than on the street. He could wind up dead doing the things he did; at least in jail he had some protection and some electricity. He had gotten so bad that he was robbing people and convenience stores at gunpoint. This was the point in my life when I really began to understand what was going on around me and within my family. I can remember my mother saying, "That's what his a-- gets," or, "His a-- should not be in the streets f---ing up." When she would talk about my brothers, it was hard for me to listen because it made me realize where we stood in my mother's eyes. We were nothing more than a burden to her. Imagine your parents feeling like you are an obligation rather than a blessing, and then multiply that by a 1000, and that was our reality every day. I remember thinking, if they don't protect us, who will? Initially this weighed heavily on my heart, but over time, I became immune to her neglect and no longer jumped when she cried.

My mother and father didn't take responsibility for their children, so my brothers and I had to raise ourselves. We had no other immediate family, other than my grandmother, to turn to because my mother only had one brother and he was in the same situation as her. My father's side of the family did not want to have anything to do with us, so we rarely visited them. They figured we weren't their responsibility. "Why bother?" Unless they were going to get money out of the deal, they didn't want anything to do with us. They had their own problems, and we had more than our own share of them.

I WANT TO GROW

Can I grow to be what I desire?
Can my dreams become realities, or do I have to continue to
burn in ghetto's fire?
Can I reach for the stars and as far as the outer space,
Or am I trapped in ghetto's cage and forced to live in disgrace?
Can my dreams travel outside the 'hood,
Or am I forced to submit to crime because you told me there
was no way I could?
Can I become a lawyer, an educator, or even the president of
the United States,
Or should I give up and let the hood determine my fate?
Can I break the barriers that lock me in,
Or should I just give up like my friend?
Is it possible for me to break this norm,
Or are the rains too powerful for me to make it from the storm?
Should I go to school, in hopes that it creates a path,
Or should I fall to my knees and submit to ghettos wrath?
What should I do?
Been in the hood for so long I forgot the skies were blue,
Black rains have plagued my kind and me for centuries,
Got us thinking our lives our empty.

I want to grow
I want to soar
I want to explore the corners of the earth, and be released from
this life so poor.
I want to be free,
I want to be me,
A human being that controls his destiny.
I want to raise my child away from this land of crime,
I want to make sure that my child doesn't wind up doing time.

I want to defy the odds inflicted on us,
I want to live in a land where I can trust.
I will find that place,
That land of opportunity where I am not hated because of my
face.

I will pave the way for my child.
Why should he have to live like an animal in the wild?
I will be the keeper of hope,
The key that unlocks poverty's gate, so my seeds don't have to
grow up around dope.
I will rise,
Bringing with me my people, so that they no longer have to
hide.

I will be that light that has been burnt out in the ghetto since
the beginning
I will make sure we are winning.
I will grow,
Let's rise, my seeds.

Chapter Two

Living with My Grandmother

My mother, my brothers, my uncle, his family, and I, all lived with my grandmother. Travie was three, I was five, Bernard was seven, and Peanut was eight. My uncle Junior, his wife, Shawn, and their daughter, Winter, were crowded into my grandmother's two-bedroom house. My mother, brothers, and I lived in the garage. At one point, we had all stayed in the house together, but that was only until the garage roof was fixed.

Neither my mother, uncle, or aunt had a job; they all depended on welfare to help my grandmother pay the rent. They didn't have steady work, nor did they attempt to go out into the world and find a job. They knew that my grandmother would not let them live on the street, so they used her for whatever they could get. They didn't care about the strain this put on my grandmother. She was too old to handle the stress of having to take care of her two children, along with her grandchildren, and she was suffering from both arthritis and cancer. Emotionally, she couldn't afford to adopt her children's burdens in life, but she did for the sake of her grandchildre. If she hadn't been so unselfish, I don't know where we'd have been.

Even though the time we lived in my grandmother's house

was tough, we always had a roof over our heads, and that was something no one else in my family seemed to be able to do on their own. Even though my grandmother opened her home to her children, she wouldn't let them take advantage of her or her generosity. I can remember clear as day, it was early in the morning and my grandmother had just discovered that she was missing a large sum of money from under her bed. She knew my mother hadn't been in the house to take it, and the only people with access to the house were my aunt and uncle. She immediately confronted them about the money, but they denied it. She politely told them to give her the money back, but they told her they didn't have it. My grandmother always kept a gun under her rocking chair and my aunt and uncle knew it, and as they continued to deny taking the money, they slowly started heading towards the back of the house.

My grandmother said, "If my money is not returned to me this instant, I will shoot, and I will shoot to kill." My aunt and uncle didn't think she was serious, and continued to patronize her. So she grabbed her 38-caliber pistol and started shooting. She rose to her feet with the help of a cane, and fired more shots. They ran for the back door and managed to get away with their lives. I can remember standing beside my grandmother as she was shooting. I remember the fire from the gun, the bullets whistling by my head, and the sounds of pure panic, all because my aunt and uncle stole money to buy drugs.

In fact, one of the bullets went through a kitchen cabinet, through a cream jar, through the wall, and out of the house. Even though my grandmother was sixty years old, she did not play around. I was only five years old, and I stood there in shock. I didn't know how to react to the situation right away, but later that day I remember laughing at my aunt and uncle because of what had happened. I had never seen her do anything like it before, but I knew, "don't mess with grandma!" I wished we didn't have to live so close to my uncle. My uncle's appearance depended on his drug use. He was skinny when he was on crack, and a nice full-size when he was off drugs. He was an immature boy, trapped in a man's body. I didn't like him. We have all met someone like him; he was the neighborhood kid who did or said things, just to get under your skin. The kid who was threatened by the fact that you were better then him, or could be better then him, so he did everything he could to sabotage you. That was my uncle!

When I was younger, he spoke to me like I was an idiot, just to get a reaction, or he sent me to do errands for him, just because he knew I couldn't say "no." I can remember one day when he was getting drunk and high in my grandmother's backyard, he offered my brothers and me some alcohol and marijuana. I didn't know what alcohol was; I was only seven-years-old at the time. I gave it a try, and the burn in my chest was so painful that I haven't touched it since. My brothers, on the other hand, liked it, and they even smoked some weed with my uncle as well. He let them drink and smoke as much as they wanted until they were drunk and high. I sat in amazement, not because I understood what they were doing at the time, but because they could drink that awful stuff! Now, I sit in amazement when I think about what they were actually doing and the way their lives turned out. After that day, they didn't mind drinking or smoking. My uncle had created a glorified picture of alcohol and weed and managed to convince them that there was nothing wrong with it.

Like I said, my uncle tried to sabotage anyone if he thought there was a chance that he would do better than him in life. Two years ago, I spent Christmas in California with my family. We all met at my mother's house: my brothers, my father, my aunt and uncle and their children for the day. You see, Junior and his wife don't have custody of any of their children because two of them have died mysteriously. They have eight living children; and Shawn, Junior's wife, was pregnant again. So my mother arranged for all of the children to be able to come over to her house for Christmas Day. Well, the two oldest kids are at the age where they are beginning to look at going to college, and because they were wards of the court, they can have the majority, if not all, of their education paid for. As soon as Junior found this out, he began trying to convince them to move home with him. These kids were juniors in high school. They had been separated from their family for most of their lives and had lived in foster homes and apart from their brothers and sisters for years. Neither Junior nor Shawn had done anything to get them back. But as soon as Junior found out that they had a chance to go to college, he wanted to sabotage it. After all, if they got out of the 'hood, they would be able to see him for what he really was. This is the type of man he is, and when he couldn't guilt them into giving up a future, he asked me to do it. I looked right at little Huddy and his brother and said, "I wouldn't move back in with him. I would do whatever I had to, to get out of here!" Junior was pissed, but I really couldn't care less, and given that I was by then two hundred and fifty pounds of muscle, I dared him to step to me like he did when I was a child.

∾

Living in my grandmother's garage, and keeping company with Junior and his wife was no picnic! In addition to my idiot uncle, we had no heat and had to share one bed. Welfare has the power to limit a family's ambition to strive for something better. By letting it do this, my mother accepted and settled for mediocrity or less. She did not want to go out and try to find a better way of life for her children, nor did she try to encourage us to strive for something more out of our lives, like a college education, a good paying job, or a decent family structure. She was content to live in the ghetto and to do nothing with her life. My mother never attempted to change the miserable conditions in which we lived, but my brothers and I were tired of having to struggle for food and clothes. We wanted her to care for us, and we knew that it was possible, if she found a job.

I think our parents tried to convince us and themselves that things were different. At least that's what my mother tried to do in her attempt to save face. She included herself in the success of someone and something totally independent of her. But hey, that's the ghetto mentality, and it took me twenty years to forgive this selfish behavior. It wasn't all her fault; my brothers and I knew that if my father had helped my mother out, we could have had a better life. We were stuck in a financial dilemma, the only way to get out of it was through our parents and that never seemed to happen. This miserable existence continued for my entire childhood, and I learned not to say a word about it to my parents. What was the point?

We lived in my grandmother's garage for two years, then one day my mother's boyfriend burned it down because my mother no longer wanted to be in a relationship with him. Seriously, you would think that this only happened in the movies, but nope, this was our life. I mean, what kind of person burns down someone's house because she breaks up with him? What kind of woman dates a man who is on the brink of setting someone's home on fire? It makes no sense, but hey, that was our lives. Their relationship ended when my mother decided that she had enough of his abuse and no longer wanted a relationship that wasn't going anywhere. When she finally built up enough nerve, she told him, "I'm leaving you. Don't you ever come back to this house." He was so mad that they engaged in a verbal war and sparks flew. He was yelling and cursing at her, calling her all types of names. She was yelling back at him, telling him to get the hell away from the house until he stormed off in a frenzy.

Even though now I can look back and joke about it, this was one of the scariest moments in my life. Later that night while we were all asleep, this man came back over to our house and lit the garage on fire. My mother woke us up in the middle of the night with pure terror in her eyes because there were flames surrounding the entire garage. That is a scary moment for a child; not only being in a fire, but when you look into the eyes of your parent, and see that she is as scared as you are. Her ex-boyfriend had tried to cage us in by blocking the front exit with chairs and bricks, it seemed like there was no way out, and no one was there to help us escape from the inferno. I can remember as if it were yesterday; my mother cried for help with desperation in her voice as she screamed, "We can't find a way out!" I can still see her pushing on the door and yelling, "Help me!" We all tried to push the door open together but it would not budge. My brothers and I were petrified because flames were no more than an arm's length away. We could feel the heat getting hotter and hotter, and we all began to cry.

Fortunately, miraculously and thankfully, our neighbors heard our cries and rushed over to move the bricks and chairs away from the garage door. We all ran out of the garage, frantic and barely escaping with our lives. We stood back and watched as the garage burned to the ground, along with all our belongings. We immediately began spraying my grandmother's house with water so that the fire wouldn't spread, and when the fire department finally arrived, they saved my grandmother's house from burning down as well. They arrived in the nick of time. The fire from the garage could not be contained any longer, and the flames were beginning to spread. I could only think of one thing. Where are we going to stay? Then off to a motel we went with nothing but the clothes on our back.

Today when I look back on that night, I wonder how we survived. Not just that night, but our entire childhood! These were the kind of people that my mother surrounded herself with—people who could get so angry they would rather kill a family than feel rejected; people who would do anything, or sacrifice anyone, for a hit, and people with no morals and no conscience. Somehow, I am sitting here today. That is the real miracle: the children living in the ghetto survive to tell about it.

My mother had just received her welfare check and managed to save it from the fire, so we had money to live on for the time being since my grandmother's was no longer an option. Grandmother refused to let us stay in her house any longer. She was afraid that my mother's boyfriend would do to her house what he did to her garage. Everyone knew my mother's ex-boyfriend was wandering around town somewhere, and no one wanted to take the risk of him coming back. We stayed right around the corner from where my grandmother lived until the police arrested the man who had burned down the garage—our home. After his arrest, my grandmother let us move in with her until my mother found her own house.

Again, living with my uncle and his family was nothing to celebrate. My uncle was even more controlling when we moved back in with my grandmother because everyone knew she didn't really want us there. Not necessarily us (as in her grandchildren), but rather my mother. My uncle did what ever he had to, to make sure we understood that he was the boss. He was a reactionist; he reacted to our misbehavior with extreme means of punishment. He would push me to the ground, punch me, and curse at me. A large part of his anger stemmed from the fact that he did not have a stable home of his own. Even when I was younger, he annoyed me, but worse, he enjoyed hitting me. As an adult, I can't respect that and like I said, we [as children] don't forget those kinds of memories.

MY SOUL CRIES

My soul cries because innocent children are loosing their lives

I despise the demise that's been hidden the lies, which are causing
the cries in these ghetto kids eye's

I notice the injustice that's causing a disservice in the quest to
understand what our purpose really is

This system is holding us hostage because it continues to damage
our image

Now how did we manage to let the system take advantage of our
voyage through life

We continue to salvage our roots, giving up one by one, by selling
our souls like prostitutes

Now we refute and dispute against those who try to bring us out
of the dark

Illiterate to the deliberate demise from the start

Why can't we articulate the immaculate essence of black?

Embrace it, because it's in a fragile state and bring it back

Our heritage has been lost for so long that we must salvage what
remains

We must break these psychological chains, so that we may dupli-
cate, better yet, triplicate its delicate remains

Don't think for one second that our setbacks were an accident,
because this manifestation that we are living in is deliberate

We are so far gone and don't know right from wrong, that you
think my words have no validity

You think by going against this standard and following a new
path is too risky

What a pity

Don't you see that the life that surrounds you is gritty

I'm just trying to smooth out your course a bit

I am truly trying to inspire you to embrace education, so that that you don't quit

I know your world is turning and it's turning quick

But until you recognize this cycle, your world is going to make you sick

You'll die living this standard, just as you were trained

I just pray you recognize the disguised trap, so that you break the psychological chains.

Chapter Three

Distancing Myself

My brothers were the only people I had to turn to, to share life's problems with, but even we were distant from each other. Although we may have shared each other's sufferings and sorrows, we dealt with them in different ways. Bernard and Peanut had things they did together, like joining a gang, selling drugs, and robbing people. Travie was too young to gang bang, so he just played with friends, and I was left to become the loner of the family. I spent the entire day away from home in order to make money for food, clothes, toys, and most importantly, to keep my sanity.

I pumped gas, washed cars, helped people with their groceries, and even begged for money to get the things I needed and desired. Bernard and Peanut did their gang thing, Travie did his kid thing, and I got my hustle on. After I found out what hamburgers and french fries tasted like, I couldn't stand eating beans and rice anymore, especially not everyday. I knew that if I had money, I could buy the things I needed in order to survive. If I did not go out and work to make that money, I would not have been able to eat or buy the little things I needed. Therefore, I did what I had to do to survive.

I continued to put more distance between my family and myself. Everyday after school, I would go to the gas station and pump gas for quarters. I found that pumping gas gave me a place to stay away from home, and allowed me to satisfy the hunger in my stomach. There was no food at home, so I had to look for other ways to come up with a meal. I watched older people pump gas for money, so I felt that if I gave it a try I could maybe make a little money as well. The job paid well enough that I no longer had to depend on my parents to put food in my tummy. I tried to introduce my brothers to this moneymaking idea, and my brother, Bernard gave it a one-day trial period.

Together Bernard and I made four dollars and ninety-five cents, the best I had ever done. After we finished for the day, we went to the hamburger stand and ordered some hamburgers. It felt as if we were living the good life, but obviously, it wasn't that convincing to Bernard. He decided he didn't like it and went home and told my grandmother what I was doing to get money. My grandmother was furious, but I didn't let that stop me! After Bernard snitched on me, my grandmother told him to hold me down so that she could beat me with her cane to teach me a lesson, but my biological needs were a lot stronger then her swing, and I continued to pump gas everyday after school. I had to eat!

Pumping gas was never easy. I can remember the gas clerks chasing me away because they did not want me to bother their customers. This frustrated me so much because I was only there to earn money for food. I never understood why they would repeatedly chase me away from one of the only opportunities I had to earn money. That's the problem with the ghetto: you get so used to seeing poverty that you develop immunity. Rather than seeing a desperate and hungry child, they saw a nuisance. I found a way to avoid them. I would hide behind the gas pumps until a customer would pull up, and then I would ask them if I could pump their gas, staying behind the pump while awaiting a response. If they said "yes," I would stoop behind their car and pump the gas. This method did not work all the time, so I had to improvise.

When my gas business was not going well, I would ask people for money so that I could buy some food for myself. My most effective slogan was, "Excuse me ma' am, today is my birthday. Can I have quarter to get some food?" I knew the value of a dollar at a young age, and if I didn't want to continue to feel that pain in my stomach, I needed to go out and do whatever it took to earn money.

My brothers never understood why I did these things, so they never joined me. They would rather sit at home and mix flour and water together to make some "pancakes." Do you know what flour and water makes besides pancakes? Glue! Or they would rather pick roaches out of the cereal and eat them with powdered milk than earn their own money. I could not sit in that house and listen to my family complain about every little thing, nor could I continue to be the target of my uncle's anger. I had to get out to survive, and the only way I could do that was by pumping gas and begging for money. I was only six, but I did what I had to.

Even though I spent the majority of my time at a gas station or at a local market begging for money, I still found a little time to hang out with my brothers and get into all kinds of trouble. When I was six years old my brothers, our friends and I, went to a park to hang out. We came across a bag of school supplies, which had been stolen by a notorious local gang, who happened to be Crips. We agreed not to go near the bag because we did not know where the gangsters were, but there's always someone who pushes the envelope. Anyway, one of our friends went over to the bag despite our warning and like idiots, we followed. We began looking through the bag and sorting out what we wanted to keep, until we heard someone say, "Get the hell out of our bag!" We all looked at each other, then as the gangsters came toward us, and we took off running. I can remember feeling as though we were never going to escape and that they were going to beat us to death, but we split up and all went in different directions.

I went with my brother Peanut and we made it home safely, but when we went back to check on our brother Bernard, we saw him in the alley pretending that he was dead so that the gang members would not bother with him. As we stood behind a wall and watched him lying in the alley, we tried to get his attention, but it was too late, the gang had spotted him. They came around the corner, walked up to him, and kicked him to see if he moved. When he did not, they left him alone and went to look for the rest of us. We stood there until the coast was clear and told Bernard that they were gone. I can remember feeling relieved to find out that everyone made it back to our street safely because I honestly thought that we were going to die that day.

After that, we all went home for fear that they might still be hunting for us. When my brothers and I arrived home, we found my mother and grandmother on the couch crying because my grandmother was being forced to sell her house. The bank was threatening to foreclose if she did not pay them, and we were forced to move again when my grandmother sold her home.

THE GHETTO CRY

Deep in the heart of the ghetto
We search for peace and tranquility, somewhere that is mel-
low.
This desire lurks deep within our subconscious
Yet unfortunately we know that nobody wants us.
We are the leftovers, discarded as waste
That's why they gathered us up and put us in the cruel, cruel,
place.
It's hard to find us in this dense fog, but yet we still exist
We are here in the pitch black dark and in the early morning
mist.
If you chop through the fortress, you'll find us deep in the
woods
You might get some bumps and scratches on the way, but you'll
find our neighborhood
It's the little poverty bubble secluded from everything else
A land with limited means, that locked away from all the
wealth.
Now when you find us, I hope the pollution in the air don't
kill you too
Because the majority of my kind is dying in the dew.
Hopefully, when you reach our destination
You'll look for solutions to end our black rain.
Our cry goes on.

CHAPTER FOUR

MOVING TO 28TH STREET

This proved to be nothing more than another obstacle I had to face growing up in the inner city of Los Angeles, Calif. I couldn't do anything about the situation my family faced, so I refused to shed a tear. I went on with my "pointless existence" and continued to do the things I had always done, until the day came when we had to leave. The biggest change was for my mother and uncle; they now had to look for their own apartments. My grandmother could no longer support them and their families. Our only saving grace was that my mother and uncle had just enough time to save enough money to make a down payment on their own places to live.

Leaving my grandmother's house meant we had to adjust to a new environment and new people. I had to adjust to a new school, make new friends, and find new methods of work. The only thing that didn't change was my struggle to satisfy my hunger. The only thing I really looked forward to was not seeing my uncle's face everyday. I no longer had to listen to him complain about how the world was against him, or how no one wanted to give him a job. I no longer had to be the target of his anger, and that made me feel great. I knew that my family couldn't be in any worse condition than the one we had previously faced, so I didn't worry about the change. I was ready to take on new challenges and even embraced the move from my grandmother's house.

My family and I relocated to a duplex building on 28th Street and Vermont. My grandmother lived in the apartment downstairs, and we lived in one above her. This was very convenient for the family, especially for my mother, because if she needed to go out and have fun she could tell our grandmother to watch us. Although we lived directly above her apartment, we still faced the issue of having no food at times. Originally, I thought that because my grandmother lived close by that we could go down there if there was no food in our fridge; that was not the case. My grandmother put her foot down. She told my mother, "Take care of your own kids. I'm not gonna help you anymore." This new responsibility shocked and upset my mother. She responded by stomping up the stairs in an attempt to upset my grandmother with the noise she was making. How could someone dare to tell her to take care of her own children? Who could blame her? She had four kids and this was the first time she had to take responsibility for them. Is it any wonder it took me twenty years to get past my anger?

Fortunately, my uncle and his family moved to a different neighborhood, away from us all. That truly gave me an opportunity for a better life because I no longer had to put up with my uncle's bullying; we had our own apartment now. We no longer had to live under the same roof. He had his home and we had ours, and that made my life much simpler. Life even seemed a bit more comfortable because I did not have to deal with him on a daily basis. Nor did we have to live in a garage, or a house where there was not enough room for all of us to relax comfortably. There was less tension within my family because everyone had a little more space and privacy.

We lived in a three-bedroom apartment, and I loved it!

Peanut and Bernard shared a room, and Travie and I shared a room. There was still an issue of getting a decent meal every night, but I could deal with that one day at a time. We were still better off then we were before. My mother even had a new boyfriend who seemed to be nice in the beginning, until my brothers and I found out the truth... He and my mother were selling drugs.

As it turned out, my mother was one of the biggest drug dealers in the neighborhood. I first noticed that she was doing drugs when I was only seven years old. This was not only tragic, but was disastrous to my relationship with my mother. I would have never believed she was capable of doing something like that. She may not have been the most responsible parent, but at that time, I still believed she wouldn't do anything to jeopardize the lives of her children. But I was wrong, and this was just another reason for me to believe that she really did not care about what happened to us. As a young kid, I knew that there were drugs in my community, but I never thought my mother would help our neighborhood kill itself. We had people coming in and out of our house at all hours of the day and night. It was open like a twenty-four hour, seven days a week, gas station—someone always wanted to get high.

There was nothing my brothers and I could do to stop the traffic flow in the house, so we just pretended like we didn't see anything. We knew it was wrong because our school put on drug prevention programs every year, but she threatened to whip us if we told anyone. So we said nothing, nor did we ask any questions about what she and her boyfriend were doing. We went on with our lives as though nothing was wrong. Then tragedy struck, and we witnessed my mother having a seizure.

Our uncle was over smoking dope when our mother started acting bizarre. My brothers and I never witnessed my mother on the ground in convulsions before. During such a traumatic event, we could do nothing but cry out in anger. She was on the ground shaking and coughing up blood as thick as syrup. My brothers and I ran around the house crying and hitting the walls because we were frustrated and did not know what to do. My uncle tried to hold her tongue down so that she wouldn't swallow it. We thought she was going to die. Fortunately, she survived, but she was delirious for a while. After calming down, she had a fixed look on her face, she was daydreaming about something. She would not move or say anything, which scared us even more because we did not know if she was going to go into convulsions again or not. "What happened?" I remember asking my uncle.

"She had a rock of cocaine the size of a marble in her mouth!" He said, "She was choking on it during the seizure. That's why she coughed up all that blood." This is when I found out that not only was my mother selling drugs, but she was also smoking crack.

My uncle was always honest with us about drugs and using drugs, even though he used them himself. Despite the fact that he was an immature boy in a man's body, he always told my brothers and me what was going on in my mother's life, and he told us that she was high when she had her seizure. This dictated a whole new lifestyle for us; we now were in the presence of someone who would steal and do anything she could to get her fix and - worst of all - that person was our mother.

Her crack addiction destroyed me because it caused so much pain. I could not believe that on top of not having food in the house, or clean clothes on our backs; my brothers and I had to deal with a mother on crack. The little respect I had for her was gone, and I refused to even look at her face. I despised the woman that called herself my mother, and I did not care if she was dead or alive. After all, what difference did it make if she just walked around like a zombie looking for a fix?

We made fun of crack heads in school, and now my mother was one of them. I was embarrassed when she had to come to school because of my discipline problems. I did not want anybody to see her because they knew that she was a crack addict. The word had circulated through the neighborhood. Although she never came to the school high, everyone knew that she was an addict, and my friends would make fun of her. I could not defend her because it was true. I absorbed the ridicule, but occasionally it led to fights. I couldn't contain the anger I felt about my family life and when the time presented itself, I acted out with bursts of anger directed at my peers and at my teachers.

My mother's boyfriend started beating her when she smoked his crack. I can remember waking up and hearing her begging her boyfriend to stop hitting her. "Please, stop!" My brothers and I were too young to do anything about it, but we tried to protect her regardless. Together we broke my mother's bedroom door down and started covering her up with our bodies. He finally stopped beating her and left. This did not work all the time, but during this particular incident, it seemed to do the trick. Her face was bloody and she had a black eye. We all started crying because we couldn't do anything to prevent him from hitting her again. I remember my feelings, I feel helpless; I have no way of saving her from this "intruder." Even though I felt motherless, I still loved her, and the fact that anyone would even consider hurting her in any way, whatsoever made me furious. Part of me wanted to kill him.

This incident led me to realize that I did not want to become a man like him. I felt the pain that he inflicted upon my family and did not want to be responsible for inflicting that same pain on another family. Emotionally, this helped me realize how not to act as an adult with a family. This man abused his power as a man by hurting my family both physically and emotionally.

My mother was so heavy into selling crack that word spread to addicts everywhere that they could get their next fix at my house. With this growing popularity in the drug business, it was not long before the police found out. I can remember as clear as day, hearing a knock at the door early one morning. I was eight-years-old and did not have a clue about what to expect. Everybody was asleep except for me, and I was unaware that this day would change the way I viewed the police for the rest of my childhood. I went to the window to see who it was, and to my surprise, it was a police officer pointing a 45-caliber pistol at me. He said, "Open the door, son."

"Mom!" I called.

He continued yelling, "Open the damn door, Boy."

I screamed for my mother as loud as I could, but she still did not hear me. With his weapon still pointed at my face, he said, "Son, if you don't open the door, I will have to shoot you."

This scared me and I had a feeling in my gut that the police officer was about to shoot me at any minute. It was petrifying to know that at any second I could lose my life, so I pretended like I was going to open the door and hid out of the officer's range of vision.

There was no way he could shoot me now because he could not see me. I started yelling for my mother and the police officers proceeded to bust the door down. I ran to my mother's room in a panic and told her what was going on, but before she could get up, they were already in the house. My mother had to wait for the cops to order her to get on the ground. The police ordered all of us to lie face down on the floor and not to move. They handcuffed us all and took us outside on our front lawn, with my brothers and me on our knees in our underwear, while my mother was in the police car answering questions from an officer. It was very cold that morning and the grass was covered in mist. My brothers and I were freezing. We were looking at each other with puzzled expressions on our faces. The police tore apart our apartment searching for drugs. They found some and arrested my mother. Fortunately, my brothers and I were able to move into my grandmother's apartment just downstairs.

I can remember looking around and seeing all our friends and their parents outside of their houses watching the police take our mother to jail. They saw how the officers tore our house apart and glared at us as we were on our knees, handcuffed on our front lawn. I was so embarrassed that I kept my head down the entire time. My brothers did the same; we all felt ashamed and humiliated because of our situation. After the police officers left the scene, we went over to my grandmother's apartment and listened to her tell us how stupid our mother was for selling drugs.

We had to face the fact that if our friends did not know our mother was selling crack before, they definitely knew now. It crushed me, and I knew that everyone was going to start asking questions about what happened. I felt ashamed because we were already poorer than all the rest of our friends, and now, on the other hand, we were known as the drug house in the neighborhood.

Our neighbors began to notice people coming in and out of our house. One of my friends asked me, "Why did the police have you and your family on the ground in handcuffs?"

I was at a loss for words, so I made up a lie, "Someone planted drugs on my mother and lied and said that she was a drug dealer."

He took what I said to be the truth, and went on about his business. I feel like all of them have their eyes on me. No matter what I do, they look down on my family. I feel worthless and bitter towards my neighbors. The bitterness turned into hatred, resulting in me no longer talking to most of my friends in the neighborhood.

At the same time, some people knew what it took to survive in the 'hood. They did not fault my mother for what she did because it was a norm. Many people in the 'hood sold dope, but my mother was one of the largest drug dealers around, and that put a spotlight on my family. Eventually everyone accepted her new way of making money and no longer questioned my family's way of life. Everyone went on with their pointless lives, and tried to make the best out of their situation. My mother spent over one year in jail and during that time, my grandmother had custody of my brothers and me.

As my home life deteriorated, my life at school felt the relentless wrath of crack as well. The problems at home did not stop there; I carried them to school with me everyday. Without even knowing it, I used school as an escape from my chaotic life at home.

Young Soul

I came into this world free of mind and unaware of life's destiny.
Born into a society that's been manifested by the majority,
I had no clue that my society was designed for me to fail,
It was designed to keep me locked in and never to prevail.
Yet my young soul was oblivious to the facts,
I had no clue on how the outside worked so I followed my pack.
I joined the cycle and had no clue on my fate,
I had no idea I was sealed behind this steel gate.
I looked at it as a way of life,
The norm, so I guess it had to be right.
I had no guidance,
Because the people I looked up to were pride-less,
They were broken by the ills of history,
That to my lost soul, was a mystery.
Yet I continued towards my clouded dreams,
To have a car, some clothes, and a beautiful queen.
In my world this is what you died for,
It was the journey you couldn't wait to explore,
Education wasn't part of the plan,
It only slowed you down, limiting your chances to get all you can.
Cursed because you couldn't find a good job,
Didn't want to work at a fast food restaurant, so innocent people you'll start to rob,
Now the cycle continues to grow,
It welcomed another lost soul, who was oblivious and didn't know.
Now I'm in the trap,
Yet unaware of it, I continue to open that gap,
The young lost soul only knows what he see,

Unfortunately, it's a clouded destiny.
Yet the days go by and a change never occurs,
Only coming to the reality that society's morals have been blurred.
The young lost souls have been captured by the tornado of hate,
Consumed by the ghettos manifested destiny, that's got me concealed behind poverty's Gate,
Though my struggle still goes on, I will never be aware because I'm blinded by a Manifested vision, That convinces me not to care.
My blind state of mind.

CHAPTER FIVE

THE WORST KID IN THE CLASS

From second grade until I graduated from high school, I was on the honor roll for perfect attendance. I rarely missed school. Even when I was sick, I tried to go. Why? Because at school I had two meals a day and did not have to listen to my family fight all the time. Yet I still took my frustrations out on my peers and my teachers, frustrations that stemmed from my family, and continued to grow inside me until I left for college. The negativity and poverty surrounding my family made me miserable. I hated the continuous feeling of hunger grumbling in my stomach. I hated the ridicule that I faced from my peers about the clothes that I wore everyday. I found myself fighting all the time: fighting with other students, fighting with my teachers and fighting with myself. Even though being at school was better then being at home, it still came with its own set of consequences.

I remember screaming at my teachers if they tried to belittle me in front of the class. I fought my peers because they made fun of the clothes I wore, and I was an overall problem for everyone who crossed my path at school. This is how I released all of the pent up aggression regarding every aspect of my life! I was a time bomb and whenever someone at school did even the smallest thing to light my fuse, there was an explosion. I took every negative aspect of my life that was occurring at home, and I vented it on the people around me. I couldn't bear the pain of my family and my lifestyle on my own, so I tried to inflict that same pain I was feeling on my teachers, peers, and anyone else around me.

There was no controlling me! I would try to do the right thing and not act up in class, but to me it felt like people intentionally wanted to piss me off; and when my teachers tried to discipline me, I let it all out. I screamed obscenities at them like, "F--- you!" or "Shut up, b----!" and when they tried to punish me, I ran my fingernails down my face and tried to scratch off all the skin. Hence, teachers suspended me constantly and then someone at home punished me, and probably rightfully so. It's sad that I can look back and realize my own cries for help in some of the most stereotypical ways! Suspension did not suppress or cure my attitude; it fueled my frustrations and anger because it put me back in the environment I hated so much. At that time, no one in the world tried to reach me, or tried to help me manage my situation. I was on my own and I had no one to turn to for help. No one had time for a problem child. They had to attend to the other kids in school, and I was becoming more and more of a burden.

I can remember a time when I was only eight or nine and I was so miserable that I dug my own grave in my backyard. I told my family, "I want to die." When my mother used to whip me, I got so angry that I did things to try to hurt myself. One day, I tried to kill myself. I climbed onto the garage in our backyard and jumped off so that I landed flat on my stomach. I leapt off the roof and did a belly flop onto the dirt. When I landed, I thought I was dead for sure, but to my surprise, I was very much alive and hurt. I was so pissed that I didn't die because the pain was excruciating. I was in so much pain that my ribs, head, knees and shoulders all hurt, but the greatest pain was felt in my heart. God did not release me from the pain I felt every day and I never understood why. What makes this story so horrible is that as an adult when I reminisce on my childhood with my mother, she thinks this is one of the most hilarious memories. Not even now, sixteen years later, does she understand that her eight-year-old would have rather been dead then live the life he was living with her.

I went to school to escape the madness, but I did not realize that I brought my problems with me. Since I needed someone to vent my frustrations on, I vented at school both mentally and physically. I became incredibly disruptive in the classroom, which resulted in suspensions from school on a regular basis.

I remember my teacher once said, "Get out of my class and go to the principal's office. You're distracting the class." I became so irate that I grabbed a chair and threw it at her. I was so mad because I knew that the principal was going to suspend me from school and make me go home, and I didn't want to go. I resented my teacher for not understanding that, and for not seeing me as a person who needed help. Every time she would react to something I did, it only intensified my anger towards her and the class. I resented being at home so much that I could not control my behavior anymore. I needed to vent and there was no one at home on whom I could take out my frustrations, so I became even more physically violent at school. I knew it was wrong, and I knew that I should try to behave myself, but the negative emotions that continued to build inside me were too strong.

The principal did his job and suspended me from school. When he sent me home, I became a burden on my family, which increased my punishments tenfold. Eventually, whippings from my mother and uncle stopped affecting me because I found ways to hurt myself more than they could. I wanted to show them that they couldn't do anything to hurt me or punish me because I inflicted more pain on myself. It was a way of lashing out and trying to gain control. After they whipped me, out of frustration, I would claw the skin off my face or hit myself. To teach me a lesson, my mother would get upset and whip me again, and I continued to abuse myself as soon as she finished. I didn't want her to feel any gratification from doing something to hurt me, so I repeatedly proved to her that I could do far worse to myself than she ever could.

After a while, she teased me about the way I reacted when I received a whipping, and she encouraged my brothers to do the same. She practiced her idea of reverse psychology so that I would stop; she figured if they thought it was a joke, then I would stop because I did not want them to laugh at me. It didn't work. Out of frustration, I would hurt myself even more. I was different from everybody else in my family; no one related to the pain I was going through. So I tried to distance myself from them even more because they accepted the lifestyle we lived in, when I refused to.

No one understood my pain and no one was willing to listen to me. The problems I faced were overwhelming to a child. No one was willing to try to understand the psychological affects of my home life, so I tried to get attention in any way I could. I continued to disrupt classes and the principal continued to suspend me. Eventually, they decided to put me in special education classes where they sent the mentally disabled students.

I spent 5th through 8th grade in special education. It only fueled my fire even more. I felt like I had even more freedom to act out in class. My teacher, Mrs. Jones, seemed to care about me, and she made me feel like I was accomplishing something in elementary school. When I did well, she praised my good work. When I did poorly, she punished me, explaining why I was being punished. She also told me that if I continued to act the way I did, I would never amount to anything, and I would wind up in a gang or in jail. She convinced me I was headed down a path that would lead nowhere, and I told her that I would do better as soon as I got to junior high school. She laughed and said, "We'll see." Her response upset me because it made me feel like she believed that I was not going to amount to anything. She made me feel worthless, and almost convinced me that I was going to be nothing more than a product of my environment. She believed that I was either going to be dead, or in jail, by the time I reached junior high school. Throughout elementary school I held on to the idea that as soon as I reached junior high, that life would be easier for me and so I eagerly awaited the change.

My family situation did not change, and no matter how I tried to fight it, it always maintained its control over me and my emotions. I could not escape the drugs or the hunger that surrounded me every day. Other kids constantly reminded me how poor I was; kids would come to school with name brand clothes on and look at what I wore and laughed. They knew I was poor because I wore hand-me-down clothes, while they wore new ones everyday. So I tried to do something about it myself.

No one heard my plea for help, so I quit asking. I pumped gas to put food in my stomach. I begged for the money to buy a new pair of shoes. I helped people with their groceries to buy the toys I wanted. I sold baseball cards that I stole from my teacher to survive. The value of a dollar was clear to me, and the way to get it was becoming even clearer. I even started working in my elementary school cafeteria so that I could get a little extra food each day.

I arrived at school around 6:30 a.m. so that I could help prepare breakfast for the students, and when I was done, I ate all I wanted. This served as another outlet for me to escape my life at home. My mother never asked me where I was going because she was still asleep when I left the house. Before I went to work, I would play the piano in the school auditorium because it eased my mind and made me feel as if I was the only person in the world. Everything around me came to a stop. I never had lessons, so I played from memory. Yet even my releases couldn't keep terrible things from happening to me.

THE NEGLECTED CHILD

O God, why am I ignored?
My Lord why are there so many things around me that I can't
afford?
Father, why so many people walk around me as if I didn't
exist?
Why do they mistreat me out of bliss?
What did I do to be trapped in the system?
Growing up without love, this soon turned into frustration.
Look at the miserable conditions I have to face,
Little infants growing up on the streets with blood marked on
their face.
Look at the hunger that grows daily,
Look at the pain in the eyes of these little babies.
It's crazy.
Yet for so long too many people neglected to raise me,
Now I must fend on my own,
I must take on the life of an adult, so as an infant I am grown.
Lord, look how so many of my kind grow up in hate,
Our little infants running into stone walls that turn them
away from a road that's straight.
Lord, help us out here.
There's too many of us little kids living in fear,
Give us a hand and guide us out of this mess.
We are tired of living this stressed out ghetto life, that's filled
with unhappiness.
This thug life mentality is not what we dream for,
We want to escape this madness, so Lord please show us the
door.
We need hope
Because so many of our kind is giving up, and in turn are
grabbing a rope.
So that they can end this tragedy that they face,

So that they escape the pits of hell, this cruel, cruel place.
For so long the black rain has hidden our sunshine and turned
us to hate,
Lord, please come save us from this manmade fate,
Before another child dies.

CHAPTER SIX

CHILDHOOD NIGHTMARE

This is probably one of the most difficult chapters that I wrote in this book. I never told anyone before—not even my mom, or my brothers. I remember clear as day, although it happened late at night. It was around 9 p.m., and I was on my way home from pumping gas. After picking up something to eat at a place which was directly across from the gas station, I walked a different route home than usual. Instead of going down 28th Street, I went down 27th right by a Catholic Church. On the corner as I turned, there was a hidden doorway by the church. Surrounded by darkness, no one would see anything, if someone pulled you into that doorway. I was so tired that I just wanted to go to sleep. As I was walking, somebody yanked me by that door. It was a big lady who held my head and poked something sharp into neck.

"If you say one word, I'll stick this screwdriver through your neck. If you say one word, I'm gonna stick your hand."

I was so scared, but every time I pulled away, she stuck the screwdriver deeper and deeper into my neck.

As I tried harder to pull away, she said, "If you pull away one more mother f-ing time, you'll lie here dead and nobody will know what happened." So I stopped pulling and she released some of the pressure.

"Get on your knees," she told me.

I hesitated for a moment, she pressed the screwdriver tighter, and she took my hand. "Put your hand on my skirt."

I was scared and all I could think about was the horrible smell that came from her, especially where she wanted my hand. It was a very distinct foul stench. She was trying to make me rub her in certain places. Every time I wouldn't rub the right place, she would poke my neck again.

"Please, stop."

She kept making me do it and tears rolled down my face. No one walked by. Eventually she got bored and she sat down when I was still on my knees, facing her with her legs wide open. Now the screwdriver pierced under my chin.

"Now I want you to put your face down there and ---- it."

I looked at her and said, "What?"

"---- it."

"---- what?"

"You know what the heck I'm talking about."

"I don't know."

"Lick my mother f-ing -----."

I started crying more and she said, "Shut the f--- up." I pretended I was submitting and someone walked by. "You better not say one word."

I wanted to scream but I was so afraid of getting the screwdriver in my neck.

She kept whispering to me that she would kill me. She waited until the person walked by and she continued with her demands.

"I want you to ---- it."

I was screaming in my head. God, what did I do to deserve

this? God, what did I do?

Finally, I got close and the smell was so rancid that I jumped up and she slammed by head against the brick wall. She said, "You think I'm playin'? You do that again, I'm gonna stick you and leave."

I kept thinking, I can't do this. How can I get away?

"Now, get back on your knees."

Time passed so slowly. She put my hand back and told me to start rubbing again. She got bored and pushed my head down. I got really close to where she thought I was and I got up and sprinted home. No one was there. I went in my room and went to sleep, hoping I would forget about it.

This incident has been eating at my soul. I never saw that woman again, and I always walked down my street after that. I never walked near a wall and I always tried to walk on the edge of the sidewalk, looking behind me. I just went back home to the stress of my family life. As if drugs and poverty did not bring enough tension, we had to worry about fights between my uncle and my mother.

LIBERATION

*I've been struggling on my feet throughout the heartbeat of my
life
Fighting for a way out, trying to survive
Through my bumps and bruises came walls of hate
Growing stronger and stronger as I stay looked behind this
gate
These ills inflicted on my and my folks, fall out of the sky like
hell storms
Hitting our pride enabling us to reform
So we begin to accept our fate
Our broken down dreams enables us to liberate
As our storm grows and the clouds grow thicker
Our gray skies shade our vision of a life that's richer
How can we liberate to something that's new
When the road we travel doesn't have clear way through
It's filed with nails that puncture our chance to reach our des-
tination
Causing a hesitation in our chance for liberation
Where can we find a clear path?
It's hard 'cause our world has to face inequalities wrath
We have to endure this economical gap
Yet try to liberate without a map
Traveling, lost
With our future to pay the cost
We've tried to persevere
But they constantly try to make up new laws, to keep us locked
in here
All we ask, is for liberation, a revolutionary leap towards an
equal chance at life
Yet you continue to try and confine*

Do you think we're blind
Fine, I'll help guide my folks through the hypocrisies of liberty
A lie, which tortures the sacredness of our community
Let me bring light to this situation
A situation that has existed since we were on the plantations
We were lied to and convinced that we were less than ?
Locked in a cage, so that our lives end up short
Yet this wasn't enough
We found gaps in the design, which able some of us to get out of the rough
But you just moved high up on the hills
To escape the floods of poverty, and these so called devilish thrills
Yet through the inconsistencies of the 'hood, we found another loophole
Which gave us the power for our destiny to control
Let these walls fall

CHAPTER SEVEN

FAMILY DISPUTES

One Saturday morning, I woke up to my mother and uncle arguing.

"Did you smoke my crack?"

"What are you talkin' about?"

"I know you smoked up, Junior." She walked into the bathroom where my uncle had been for over an hour. "I can smell the crack in the air."

She saw that he was high on her drugs, and she was livid. The argument escalated to the point that they got into a fistfight. My uncle punched my mother in the face and he was on top of her, punching hysterically, while she lay on the ground covering it helplessly.

My brothers and I stood nearby urging my uncle. "Please, get off her," but he refused to listen. He kept hitting her as if he could not control himself or his anger. Every time we attempted to pull him off, he shoved us away, and they started fighting again. By this time, our neighbors gathered outside to see why my mother was screaming about. They all watched and looked out their windows at the entertainment my mother and uncle gave them. I was only in elementary school at the time and all I could do was watch. Eventually he stopped and headed downstairs to my grandmother's apartment to escape the insanity.

My mother rose to her feet, dazed and with a bloody and bruised face. She grabbed a coffee cup from the kitchen and headed for the balcony to catch my uncle before he made it to my grandmother's apartment. The neighbors watched the fiasco that was taking place in our apartment, and it seemed like they were enjoying every minute of it. It pissed me off to see my neighbors enjoying the sight of my bloody, troubled mother. She made it to the balcony of our apartment and with the coffee cup in her hand, she yelled, "Junior!" As he looked up, she threw the cup as hard as she could and busted his nose. He fell to the ground in pain, yelling, "I'm going to kill you, b----!" Blood spilled all over the sidewalk and the paramedics had to come to our apartment and stitch him up.

As I turned to the people watching this brutal spectacle, I yelled, "What the hell are you looking at? This is none of your business." I was pissed! I could not believe that seeing my family hurt one another amused them.

It hurt me to see my mother and uncle fight like this; they were supposed to love each other. This made me hate them even more. My mother and uncle became nothing more than two adults I had to obey when they asked me to do something. I no longer looked at my uncle as an uncle, or my mother as a mother. They were nothing more than two people in my life.

I knew that their fight was not going to end that day because despite the fact that they always made up, they still hated each other. I never knew why they did, but they did regardless, and I couldn't change their feelings for each other. Maybe they hated each other because it was like looking in a mirror and seeing their own reflection, which was enough to upset anyone. Another time, my uncle and mother were fighting over drugs and she locked him out of her apartment. My uncle had apparently wanted to use my mother's crack pipe and she refused to let him. He became so outraged that he started threatening her again. "I'm gonna break this window if you don't open that door and give me a puff." She refused again and he threw rocks at the window where I was trying to sleep. In fact, I was taking a nap right under it and Bernard woke me up just as my uncle broke the window. I heard the glass break as I awakened, and I opened my eyes to my body covered in shattered glass, but luckily, it did not cut me.

This made my mother upset, and she ran out of the house with a butcher's knife and began chasing my uncle, trying to cut him. He took off running so my mother threw the knife at him, but missed by about a foot. Aware that she had thrown the knife, my uncle turned around and started chasing her. He caught up to her and started beating her up. Here we go again, is what I thought as he pounded away at my mother's face. There was a fight, an audience, and once again, blood was shed from my mother's face. No one on the block was willing to pull my uncle off her, so he continued to beat her. I was livid at my uncle and from that point on, I strongly disliked and ignored him whenever he was around.

My uncle and I did not agree on anything. I felt like he treated me differently from the rest of my brothers. He wanted to teach me a lesson about being a man and taking responsibility, but he did it in a way that made me hate him even more. He tried to embarrass me in front of my friends by yelling at me, or pushing me when he wanted me to do something. He was always trying to make me look stupid in front of my peers because he felt like I needed to be "toughened up." He thought I tried to get attention by making everyone think I had a problem when I really did not, so he thought it was up to him to beat that problem out of me. He tried his best to make me change my ways, but it never worked. The only thing he taught me was what kind of man I didn't want to be.

Unfortunately, my uncle played a large role in my life. He was always around the apartment because my grandmother lived just downstairs from my family. When my mother was tired of disciplining me for my wrongdoings in school, she sent my uncle to do the job for her. He whipped me and enjoyed doing it. I can remember an incident when I was in the front yard and I said something derogatory to him. He lost his temper and slapped me in the back of the head so hard that I hit the ground. I turned around and gave him an evil look, so he slapped me again, and I hit the ground again. I popped up off the ground and I looked at him in an evil way again. He became furious and with his fist balled up, punched me in the chest so hard I fell back to the ground. All my neighbors, once again, watched as he shoved me to the ground. I tried to stand up every time because I was not going to let him think that he got the best of me. After a few more times of him pushing me to the ground, he finally realized that I was not going to submit to him. He eventually gave up trying to prove his point and told me to go upstairs and go to bed. I believed that I won that battle, and from then on, I welcomed any other challenges my uncle dared to put forth. I knew I was only eight-years-old, but I was more mature than my age.

My uncle was my worst enemy, and the only way to

avoid him was not to be at home when he was around. He was one of the toughest obstacles I have ever had to overcome in my life; he was verbally and physically abusive. He didn't like me, I didn't like him, and it was mutually understood. I finally started ignoring his smart remarks. This only infuriated him even more, so he tried to discover new reasons to spank me.

I started leaving the house as soon as I saw him pull up in his car. He would see me leaving and not say a word. I would stay away from the house for as long as I saw his car parked in front of it, just so I did not have to be confronted with his negativity. I remember thinking that he had a personal vendetta against me and I couldn't say exactly what it was. I tried my best to stay away from him, even if it meant I had to stay at the gas station, or stand in front of the grocery store carrying people's groceries to their car for an extra hour or two. If I was making a little money while I waited for him to leave, the day was at least that much better.

THE CHOICE

They say I have a choice to succeed or go astray
Well here are my choices on any given day.
I attend school, with hopes to learn
So that one day I could get a job and money I will earn.
Yet, my hunger grows and money I lack,
The choices are given to me and one of them is to sell crack.
Education will help me, in time I'll see,
But will I survive today, who knows where I'll be.
I am caged in a world that has very little.
I can't seem to break free, I still can't crack the riddle.
What must I do?
I'm so confused, so I look for comfort from my crew.
We all share the same pain,
At the age of eleven we started realizing life was not a game.
So we look for ways to try to survive,
Start selling crack, jacking people, and had to hide.
The system showed us how to work.
We get a little hungry; need some clothes so we jack a jerk.
Hopefully no one ends up dead
Because loosing a little homey is the day we all dread.
My choices are simple and plain,
Get an education, be broke and in pain.
Or satisfy my needs and start selling crack cocaine.
What kind of life is this?
Where I can't eat a decent meal or have a pot to piss?
Why can't I be free, liberate my mind, and escape from poverty?
Why?
Because my choices are limited, so I don't have a chance to fly.
They stuck me in this ghetto, in the ills of the hood,
Knowing that it raises its youth to be no good.
It leads us straight to jail,
Transporting us from a hell into an even darker parallel.

Why me, what did I do to deserve this mess?
Born black, into a world that's oppressed.
But is it my fault, that the Lord gave me this beautiful skin?
Born into a world where my skin is a sin.
Well I pray to you my Lord, take me away,
Liberate my soul; please Lord right away.
My choices are slim and that's a face,
I was born into a ghetto and hated cause I'm black.
The choice is mine and that's the illusion.

CHAPTER EIGHT

MAKING MONEY

Once I found some crack in my mother's bedroom and sold it to an addict who was a regular customer at our apartment. It was the easiest money I had ever made and it came fast too. I was young but I knew the feeling of making fast money. I sold $100 worth of crack to him and I went to the store and bought some shoes, a pair of pants, a shirt and some food. I felt like I was the luckiest person in the world because it took me 10 minutes to make $100. Even though it felt good in that moment, I still feared the repercussions, so I went back to pumping gas, washing cars, helping people with their groceries and begging for money. At this point in my life, I knew how to make crack, sell crack, and even smoke it if I wanted. But I saw the power of crack and what it does to a family, and I didn't want to follow in the same path as my parents.

I felt that if I consumed myself with trying to make money my own way, I could keep away from drugs and working gave me direction. I felt responsible for my own survival and if I wanted to eat, I had to work. I knew my parents would not feed me all the time; they had lives of their own that did not include the well being of their children. I knew that if I waited around for someone to give me a handout I would probably starve to death. I realized that I needed to get on my own two feet and work to feed myself. I did not choose to be in the position I was in; I was forced into it, and I had no choice but to make the best of my situation and fight through my hard times—a mentality that I still carry with me today.

Although I was independent, I was human. There were times when my friends would come to the gas station at which I was pumping gas with their parents, and I would hide because I was worried that they would tell everyone at school. They never discovered me. If a friend saw me and confronted me, I told him that I was waiting for my mother or my brother across the street. Life at the gas station had its inconveniences. The continued confrontations with the gas station attendants caused more downs than ups.

Therefore, I developed a strong desire to sell crack because my friends glorified it. They had nice clothes, nice jewelry, and all the lunch money a person could possibly want. I wanted all of these things, but there was no way I could get them if I didn't sell crack. Elementary kids were posted on the corner selling crack to drug addicts, and their parents didn't even care. I must admit, selling crack did look alluring, but I didn't give in to the temptation.

What was the number one subject talked about among my friends? Selling crack. Most of them sold it, or were planning to as soon as they were fronted the money by a big-time drug dealer in the neighborhood. My friends knew that if they sold drugs, they would never have to worry about being broke again. They knew that if they sold crack they would have all of the newest clothes, a pocketful of money, and no worries. But I knew that they were wrong. With crack in their lives, violence was sure to follow, violence stemming from drug dealers in the neighborhood who were territorial. If someone came into their area of work, they were willing to protect themselves, and their area of operation, by any means necessary.

A friend of mine named Anthony trespassed on another drug dealer's territory to sell crack to his customers. As a result, Anthony was murdered in broad daylight in front of his auntie's house. Anthony didn't respect the boundaries of another dealer's business and paid for it with his life. His death could not be prevented; he broke the fundamental rule of the drug dealing business and knew the consequences. Though we mourned for Anthony's loss, life went on in the neighborhood, and my other friends continued selling drugs.

Selling drugs was the norm and a large portion of the population embraced it, so it was not a shock to us when someone died over selling crack. No one was influential enough to change my friends' minds and stop them from selling drugs; they were too engulfed in that way of life and couldn't see a way out.

I could not bear to go through the same thing my mother went through because of drugs. She went to jail, her boyfriend beat her, and she used the same drug that she sold. Again, she focused more on drugs than she focused on their children; I refused to walk in the same path because I knew it would only bring more pain and destruction.

Even though I was surrounded with the temptation of selling crack everyday, I was also bombarded with the deaths of friends and family as a result of selling drugs.

One Sunday afternoon, my friend Jason and his girlfriend, Elizabeth, were waiting for their bus at the bus stop. I wanted to go up to him to say hi, but business was booming, so I was too busy to go across the street. He was a member of my brother's gang and had his rag hanging out of his back pocket. I remember thinking he was crazy because the traffic was so heavy at the intersection that someone from a rival gang would definitely confront him about the rag. I continued pumping gas for a lady who had a car full of children. I doubted she would give me a tip for my services because her kids kept pissing her off, but to my surprise, she gave me a dollar. I remember how excited I was because I could then go over to the local fast food restaurant and get some food.

As I started to walk to the next customer, I heard a car slam on its brakes. I turned towards the noise and saw a car stopped in front of the bus stop with two guys hanging out the window. The sound came in an instant; six shots rang out and the car in front of the bus stop sped off. As soon as the sound of the bullets began, everyone fell to the ground for protection. I stood there in shock, as Jason and his girlfriend lay dead in front of the bus stop with blood surrounding their bodies. Jason took most of the bullets during the shooting because he jumped in front of his girlfriend and tried to save her life. Unfortunately, he could not save her and she took a bullet in the neck and one in the head. They lay motionless on the concrete with no signs of life left in their bodies; blood was pouring onto the concrete and down into the sewer. It was the first of many shootings I witnessed growing up in my neighborhood. It was so strange to me because just two minutes before they died, I saw them smiling as if they didn't have a worry in the world. I remember running home and telling my brother that Jason had just been shot. He burst into tears and left the house in a frenzy. I was so scared for the lives of my brothers that day because it could have been any one of them lying dead at that bus stop. I feared for their safety when I saw those two innocent people shot. The anxiety of death did not end with my brothers; I also worried that my mother would get caught selling drugs to the wrong person and die because of it. I could not take the chaos that surrounded me in my household, so I looked for peace and a warm meal at my friend's home.

FACTS

Nigga not, killa not, steela not,
But what do we got.
We got all odds against us.
We raised to learn not to trust,
We're born into a world of stress.
And we focus on petty things like how to dress.
Were taught to beware of our own kind,
Not to use our mind, and continue to be blind.
But the cold thing is, we don't even know.
We are like chickens with their heads cut off, and don't have
nowhere to go.
Where is our sense of direction?
I want you to step back and take a look at your reflection.
Now tell me what do you see,
It's crazy cause your reflection tells you, you don't even know
where you want to be.
But see, you not worried about that
You worried about watching your back, selling your crack,
and how much money you can stack.
But see that can only get you so far,
Yea it might get you a car
And to them young innocent ghetto kids, might look at you as
a star.
But only time will tell when I see your black a-- riding
around in the back seat of a police car
Open your eyes, you see how the system work,
Got you riding around looking like a jerk,
And at the same time got you thinking this is just work.

But on the flip side,
I'll show you how to ride, and at the same time not have to
hide.

Brotha we can do this together
And have a brotherhood that can last forever.
It ain't too late to be who you want to be,
See what you want to see,
Bratha don't give way to defeat,
Be so eager to retreat.

Look at your reflection.
Respect yourself
And have the courage to walk in a new direction.
Because the struggle continues.

CHAPTER NINE

ESCAPING TO MY FRIEND'S HOUSE

When things were more than unbearable at my house, I found myself using my friend Marcos' house as another escape. At times, my mother did not have anything in the apartment for us to eat, not even beans. We made mayonnaise sandwiches when all we had was mayonnaise and bread. We put water in our cereal when we didn't have any milk. My brothers and I tried to mix just about any and every food item together to satisfy our hunger when there was no food in the house. At times, we did not have a choice; we had to go hungry because there was nothing to eat.

A day of embarrassment was the day we got our food stamps. I was mortified if any of my friends were in the store when my mother sent me to cash-in the food stamps for change to buy cigarettes. The kids I grew up with loved to make fun of those who were less fortunate than they were because they didn't have much more than we did, and it made them feel better to put themselves above someone else. I remember keeping my new clothes in the closet for an extra week. Why? I didn't want everyone to know I got my clothes on the day the welfare checks came. On the other hand, I had no one to make fun of because we were at the bottom of the barrel.

When the weather was bad, I couldn't go out and pump gas or beg for money, so my alternative was to go over to my friend Marcos' house and play with him because I knew that soon his parents would be making a meal. Both of his parents worked and both of them made sure that their refrigerator was always stocked with food for their kids. Visiting Marcos and his family made me hate my parents even more because they didn't support us like Marcos' parents did for their family. His parents weren't so focused on getting high. I felt like my parents gave up on supporting my brothers and me. They never even attempted to look out for our well-being, so I started spending more and more time at Marcos' house.

Marcos became one of my best friends. I found myself protecting him like a brother because his family welcomed me into their home with open arms and an extra spot at their dinner table. Marcos' family knew my situation at home. They had witnessed the police officers rummaging through my house looking for drugs, the fights between my mother and my uncle, and the crack addicts coming in and out of the apartment. They felt sorry for me and helped me out quite a bit. I didn't want to wear out my welcome so I didn't go over to his house all the time. The only time I would go over to their house was when I knew I could not work at the gas station, or when business was slow. I did not want his family to think I was using them for their generosity, so I never overstayed my welcome.

There were times when Marcos needed my help as well; since I was much bigger than the kids my age, I always ended up protecting my friends from bullies. I remember an incident involving Marcos and a kid that wanted to beat him up because he didn't like him and knew that he could win if he fought Marcos. Marcos was petrified and needed my protection. I went up to the kid and I said, "Leave Marcos alone." He refused and continued picking on him. One afternoon the bully tried to take his money, but Marcos was able to run away. He came over to my house to tell me what had happened, I confronted the kid, and he admitted trying to bully Marcos. After he admitted it, we met in the back of an apartment building.

The guy started to shout-out, and act as though he wanted to fight me, so I obliged. I cocked my arm back and hit him so hard that he fell to the ground, and then he ran to get his older brother. Unfortunately for him, his older brother did not want to fight me because I had already beaten him up earlier that year. His older brother came outside and once he saw who I was, he turned around and went back into their apartment. This solidified my friendship with Marcos; he was ecstatic to know that this guy would never bother him again. After the altercation, we went to Marcos' house to eat ham sandwiches and drink juice. I loved going somewhere without the drugs and chaos. The things I took for granted—like peace and quiet—can be our greatest blessings.

I knew that the comfort would not last forever because the more I came over, the less his parents wanted me there. They told Marcos not to bring me over as much because they couldn't afford to feed me all the time. Although I was young, I knew that I was not their responsibility, and I understood why they did not want me around as much. Marcos was their child, not me. I was just the kid from across the street.

In elementary school, Marcos received good grades in every class. He was the good, well-mannered kid in the class, and his teachers loved him because he was never a problem, but over time, Marcos began to change. He went from the "nice guy," to the disturbing kid on the playground. He hung out with a local gang and they initiated him at twelve years old. He started selling drugs, stealing cars, and even participating in drive-by shootings with his gang brothers. Consumed with the ways of his street gang, he veered farther and farther away from school.

Marcos' parents could no longer control him; he had transformed from the most obedient child in class, to the most deviant child on the block, and our friendship slowly deteriorated as well. We no longer hung out together, and they seldom invited me to their house for dinner. It was strange adjusting to this new personality, considering he and I had been so close before. I remembered the kid that had aspirations of becoming a chemical engineer, but those dreams were quickly slipping from his grasp. He no longer thought about being an engineer, and the only thing on his mind was hanging out on the corner and selling crack.

Marcos' life had done a complete one-eighty, and he transformed into a person that no longer let people take advantage of him or bully him; instead, he became the bully. He carried a gun for protection at all times and was always picking fights with those around him. He no longer needed protection from me; he had a gun and an attitude to go with it. Eventually we went our separate ways. Marcos had been blessed with a loving family that took care of him, bought him clothes, and kept food on the table, but the neighborhood took control of his emotions and his parents couldn't stop him from bangin'. Marcos spent more time runnin' the streets than he did at home, and since his parents worked all the time to support him, it made it difficult for them to keep track of what he was doing at all times. The influences of the environment surrounding Marcos dictated his train of thought, causing this reaction. He conformed to the neighborhood norms: selling drugs, gang affiliations, and criminal activities.

Other friends had similar experiences to mine. They were faced with the drugs in the community, the gangs, and the poverty, too. Most of them were on welfare just like me, and their parents waited at the mailbox for their check to come on the first and fifteenth of every month. The only time my friends and I were able to get something new from our parents was on one of those two days.

In addition to the curse of the first and fifteenth, another day of embarrassment was the day we got our food stamps. I was mortified if any of my friends were in the store when my mother sent me to cash-in the food stamps for change to buy cigarettes. I remember keeping my new clothes in the closet for an extra week. Why? I didn't want everyone to know I got my clothes on the day the welfare checks came. On the other hand, I had no one to make fun of because we were at the bottom of the barrel.

I tried to take my life into my own hands by stealing from people and selling drugs, but that wasn't the life for me. The gas station was my only escape—the place where I had a role in life. There I did not have to see my parents or participate in perpetuating the negativity of my neighborhood. After making enough money for food, I bought a kite and stole some extra kite string from the hardware store so that my kite could fly even higher.

When no one was around, I went to my elementary school and flew the kite for hours at a time. It was a relaxation tool for me and gave me the freedom to think about anything. The kite symbolized freedom. I wish that I could be the kite on the end of the string, flying as high as I want, and as far away from my house as I can go. I wrapped rolls and rolls of the kite string together and let the kite soar as far as possible. I wanted to see how far it would go before I couldn't see it any more. I watched the kite soar for hours; sometimes I sat at the school until nightfall when I dreaded going home because I knew the drama that awaited me.

I had nowhere else to go. I ended up at home with all the agony that awaited me. Each night when I got up enough nerve to make the short trip home, my stomach would start to have a sick feeling. Once I let my kite go, I felt better. I want to be that kite; I want to be set free and on my own. I want to know what it feels like to soar in peace without anyone trying to hold me down. I was not that lucky, for when I let my kite go, I remained on the ground. With my head hung low, I started to make my journey home. On my way there one night, I decided that I needed to tell someone about what my mother was doing to my brothers and me; that someone would help us through our situation and put us in a home where we wouldn't have to worry about where our next meal would come from. I wanted people to understand my pain and would help us escape this lifestyle. I needed people to know what my brothers and I were going through. I needed to vent! I made the decision to tell someone, and in doing so, I changed our lives forever.

WELFARE CHECKS

We had no education, so we couldn't find work
In a time when segregation left us in the dirt.
We spoke with one voice, for equality and justice
But the majority refused, and rained injustice.
They devised a demise that broke our backbone,
They separated us economically and left us alone.
They gave us small jobs and old education,
Trapped us in a secluded society with no hesitation.
They made us feel like we got what we asked
Not knowing that it was leftovers and we were treated like
trash.

The façade that exists in this society has broken the will of my
people.

They were given well fair checks so that they were washed fur-
ther from equal.
The fallacy ran deep.
From concrete Vietnam to the pits of hell where the devil never
sleeps.
The welfare checks were a way to keep us satisfied,
It was a way to keep us out of the race and trapped in the
façade.

As we consume ourselves with this petty gift
Our young seeds grow up in poverty with no hopes for an
uplift,
As the trap grows strong.

Chapter Ten

My Mother Loses Custody of Her Children

The teacher's aide in my 4th grade class, Ms. Jackson, understood me and sincerely cared about my well-being. "Eboni, don't give up on life because your parents have drug problems. You need to strive to succeed." As the only person who listened to me, she always found time to comfort me when life became unbearable. I confessed my entire life to her, even the fact that my mother sold drugs and about the times when the police raided our house. I secretly wished that she would help ease my pain; maybe even have us taken away from my mom, but my wishes were never granted. When Ms. Jackson didn't have us removed from her custody, it made me feel even more hopeless. I began believing that we would live our entire lives in the ghetto.

One morning during class, I was called into the counselor's office. Unaware of what the topic of conversation was going to be, I was extremely nervous. I thought that I was in trouble again for something I might have done and had forgotten about. As I entered the office, a pleasant looking man greeted me. The first words that came out of his mouth were, "Welcome to my office, Eboni." Instantly, my nervousness disappeared, and I became more relaxed and ready for anything he had to say. I remember sitting in a chair directly across from his desk, and wondering, what does he want to talk to me about?

There were pictures of his family on his desk, and I thought his family looked happy, like they didn't have to worry about a thing.

The counselor began by asking me a series of questions about my mother and my family situation. Eventually he began drilling me with questions.

"Does your mother sell drugs? Is she dating someone who uses drugs?"

I replied, "My mother sells drugs, and she smokes crack. I've seen her selling crack too."

"Do you want to move out of your mother's house and relocate to a place where there aren't any drugs?"

I hesitated for a moment because I wanted to live somewhere other than with my mother, but I did not want to be away from my brothers. I wanted to live someplace where I could eat a decent meal on a regular basis, but I couldn't stand the idea of being separated from my brothers, nor did I want my mother to be mad at me because I was responsible for the police taking us away from her. So before I answered the question, I asked, "Could we stay with my grandmother, so that my brothers and I would not have to be separated?"

He agreed to my suggestion. "That would be the best."

After the conversation ended, the counselor reported what was going on in my home to the higher authorities, and so they came, took my brothers and me away from our mother, and moved us downstairs into our grandmother's apartment.

I was nervous when the county department came to take us away. They took me out of school, drove me to my mother's apartment and told my mother, "You are losing custody of your children." My mother, grandmother, and uncle were extremely upset at me for talking to a counselor about what was going on in our house.

My mother started yelling at me, "You're so stupid. You're ruining the family." She said, "I hate you, and I don't want to talk to you no more."

After she said those things, I realized what I did and I regretted it. She made me feel worthless and despite everything she did to us, I instantly felt bad for my actions. We became my grandmother's burden—her full responsibility and she had to deal with my mother and her drug habit. My grandmother knew that if she took care of us, she would pay the price; the price was my mother hanging around her apartment all the time.

Along with my mother losing her children, the apartment we lived in was taken away from her as well, and she was cut off from welfare because she no longer had custody of her children. My grandmother refused to let my mother live with her. After she lost the apartment, she began used drugs even more. Fearing that my mother would steal again to support her habit, my grandmother did not let her move into her apartment. This resulted in my mother being away from us for weeks at a time. We never knew where she was or what she did; all we knew was that she did not have a place to live. I knew she was on the street using drugs, and I couldn't help her. She did not want to be around me, and at that point, I did not want to be around her, either.

My mother always had a place in my heart, but her actions made me hate her. Sometimes I saw her out on the street corner, hanging out with her crack addict friends. Our roles were reversed—I worried for her life. How sad is it when a fourth grader pities his mother? But I did and sometimes still do. I knew that she did not have a place to go or a decent meal to eat, and it broke my heart to see my mother on the streets using drugs. There was no doubt that I had a love-hate relationship with her, a relationship that was unhealthy and unfair to us both. She should not have had to live on the streets away from her children, but she chose that lifestyle for herself.

Living with my grandmother was a lot better than living with my mother because we were blessed with a little bit more food on the table and didn't have to deal with crack addicts coming in and out of our apartment any longer. Finally, we were escaping our mother and her addiction.

Some benefits came from telling the school counselor that my mother used drugs. For example, the counselor took us to Goodwill where we received free clothes. Thrilled that my brothers and I did not have to share clothes anymore, we had a variety of them to wear and that felt great. Taking the trip to the Goodwill store made me feel like someone really did care about our well-being. Though my mother was still bitter towards me for doing such a disgraceful thing to my family—like crack is something be proud of—I still felt like I did the right thing. My mother made me feel as if I let down my entire family because I talked about the things she did at home. She refused to say a word to me. She ignored me every time our paths crossed, but I refused to take what she did to heart and let it affect me. I was hurt and felt guilty because I broke up my family, but I still felt like someone needed to speak up.

At one point, my mother tried to turn my brothers against me by telling them what I did was wrong. It worked for a while, but eventually they realized that it was the right thing to do for us because we were better off with my grandmother. Life at Grandmother's was ten times better than any life I had ever known thus far. We were free of the drugs, we were free from my mother's bursts of rage when she woke up the morning after a night of being high, and even though my grandmother was strict, she loved us. She showed us she cared by making sure food was on the table and clothes were on our backs. Even though Grandmother did not work and depended on welfare to support us, she budgeted the little money she received to take care of us. We were blessed to live with her because she offered strict discipline and guidance. We had to be in the house at a certain time and if we came home late, she would definitely remind us of our places. She was a mean lady, but she loved us a lot. She was strict but her intentions were good and she meant well. The only thing that really made her regret taking us into her house was her constant fighting with my mother.

My mother would come to Grandmother's house and make trouble by trying to force her way in to steal something to feed her drug habit. Due to this type of harassment, Grandmother almost ended up sending us to a foster home. My mother would harass her about the welfare checks she received for us, demanding that she get "her" share of the money. My mother constantly tried to move in with us, but the courts would not allow it, so Grandmother refused to let her stay. My mother eventually moved on and continued roaming the streets, finding new ways to support her crack habit.

My brothers and I saw her on the corner more than once, and we suspected that she was selling her body for drugs. We pleaded with Grandmother, "Please, let her stay in the house. She can try to get off the drugs." She finally gave-in to our pleading and welcomed my mother into her home again. Immediately after my mother moved in, she seemed like she was trying to quit, and even distanced herself from the people with whom she had been smoking crack. Her attitude changed and that made her nice to live with. Everything seemed to be going fine and life was finally getting better, but the "black rain" didn't leave my family alone for long and pain stormed back into our lives with a vengeance. The "black rain" blocked my family out of the sunshine of mainstream society and trapped us in the dark mist of the ghetto.

Eventually, my mother began to steal things from Grandmother to buy drugs again. The prison from which we thought we had escaped had entrapped us again and was trapping my grandmother as well. My mother stole Grandmother's money, her diamond bracelet, and all the rest of her jewelry. She was stripping Grandmother of everything she owned and then denied that she ever committed the acts. We could always tell when my mother was on drugs because her weight would drop dramatically and her words would become short. She would avoid us because of the shame she felt when she looked into our eyes. It was easy to tell when she tried to hide the fact that she was high; her eyes became extremely large and she zoned out for minutes at a time. There was no way my mother could hide when she was high; her body language gave it away every time.

Sometimes my mother stole all of my grandmother's money while she was sleeping. Forcing us all to go hungry because there was no food and no money, and Grandmother was stuck in a difficult situation when it came time for her to do the grocery shopping. Eventually she threatened my mother, and told her that she would give us to a foster home if she did not stop stealing from her. Out of anger my mother said, "Give the mother f---ers away and I'll never speak to your a-- again." Underneath all of her anger, my mother was scared and she eventually stopped coming by Grandmother's apartment. She stayed away and Grandmother calmed down; everything was going well again and my grandmother seemed happy.

To help Grandmother out of her financial jam, my brothers and I would go to the grocery store with a list of everything we needed to make a meal, and we were each responsible for stealing a certain item of food. We continued to steal groceries until my Grandmother was able to get enough money together to go grocery shopping for us. We always entered the store one at a time, so that the employees would not be suspicious of us. For a long time our scheme worked great, and we were able to eat a decent meal every night. We agreed that if one of us ever got caught, we would run and drop the merchandise we stole from the store so that the worker would stop chasing us.

With my grandmother constantly being a victim of my mother and her crack addiction, she began to grow more and more frustrated, and she began to take her anger out on my brothers and me because my mother was not around. This gave me an excuse to leave the house even more often than before. I started avoiding coming home until after nightfall because I knew that Grandmother would begin ridiculing me as soon as I walked through the door; not because she did not like me, but because my mother had done something to make her upset.

My mother's crack addiction tormented my life by taking the things that meant the most away from me—my family. My mother broke up our family because she did not care enough to break off her habit. She was comfortable sending her children further and further into poverty for her own self-serving reasons. My grandmother did not receive enough welfare support for four boys and my mother. My mother's constant badgering of Grandmother, made her life seem to grow grimmer and grimmer, which only made me hate my mother more. I could never understand why she constantly tried to make my life a living hell and maybe I never will.

To give my grandmother a break, my brothers and I would go to the University of Southern California's campus, and break into their candy machines and steal all the candy that we could possibly get our hands on. We filled trash bags full of candy and then walked across the street to the movie theaters. We'd sneak into a movie and sit there all day.

It broke our hearts that my mother would put Grandmother through that heartache and pain after we had begged Grandmother to help her. The pain was bad enough for us kids, but it was wrong to steal from and cause pain to an old woman who was dying of cancer. Furthermore, I could not believe my brothers and I were going through this again with my mother. I thought we had escaped this burden, but unfortunately, I was wrong. The crack was back in our lives and escaping wasn't an option.

CRACK

Move over equality, I was sent to destroy the black nation.
Bye bye education, they die for me now
They kill, steal, rob and deal, all because of me
At one point their intimate desire was to be free.
My boss's plan worked out to a tee
There were too many running free, so they sent me.
I'm a destroyer, yes, a destroyer of life.
I can make you sell your clothes, your kids, and yes, even your
wife
Try and kill me in time I'll be back
Stronger, deadlier and indeed hunting for blacks.
You ask who I am, indeed I'm not ashamed
I was sent to destroy the black nation, hello I'm Mr. Crack
Cocaine.

CHAPTER ELEVEN

CRACK COCAINE

I can remember the smell of crack as my mother smoked—a smell so dense and thick that it clogs your lungs with its distinct odor. My mother, father, uncle and auntie would sit in a room together and smoke it for hours at a time. They all had specific reactions to the drug, which became more and more obvious to my brothers and me. For example, my father could not speak when he was high; when he did, his speech was slurred and his words blended. It terrified me to see him in this state because when I looked into his eyes, I could tell he suffered from within, and he couldn't even look me in the eyes if I tried to talk to him; he was ashamed of himself.

On occasion, my father came to visit us when we lived with my mother. As soon as he arrived, they would go into my mother's room with my uncle and auntie and smoke crack together. They used this time to get high together and pooled their money to stay high. Although I was only nine years old at this point, I knew what my parents were doing when they locked themselves in the bedroom. I would deliberately ask my father questions whenever he came out; I knew that he did not want to answer me or even be around me, but I wanted him to know that I knew what they did when they locked themselves away. He would attempt to answer my questions but, as usual, he mumbled a response and his words were too jumbled together to understand.

My brothers and I giggled at my father's reaction to crack because we thought it was the strangest thing we had ever seen. My father stayed away from us when he was high because he did not want to have to talk to us. Looking back, it was the saddest thing I had ever seen because I could actually see him dying in front of my eyes. My father looked like he was going to drop dead every time he was high—his mind was in another place, and he could not comprehend many of the events that occurred around him. I can honestly say that his high was like watching someone in the twilight zone; he had no clue what was going on around him. His eyes were opened so wide, you thought that he was trying to capture the world in one glimpse.

When my uncle was high, he hummed and rocked back and forth on the couch. He sat on the it and entertained himself until his high was gone. He could speak, but he would try to avoid it, if possible. The most ironic fact about my uncle and his addiction was that I could actually respect his honesty with us about what was going on with him and my parents. He was the only one who told my brothers and me that my parents, as well as him, were using drugs. I can even recall one occasion when he said, "I wish the drug was never invented, but there's nothing I can do to get off it." He said, "The drug is calling my name and I have to answer it."

He couldn't escape the addiction because he depended too heavily on it, and whenever he tried to break his addiction, he relapsed and started using crack again. He did not want to use the drug, but his dependencies always took control of his mind, and he gave in to the temptations of crack repeatedly. I could only watch as he came closer to death.

My auntie was completely quiet when she smoked drugs. She would walk around the house chomping and sucking her teeth as though there were something stuck in them. She would try to clean everything in sight. Whenever the adults in the house got high, I became very observant. I watched everything they did and tried to make sense of what was happening around me. I watched my parents, my uncle, and auntie very closely. I knew I would never live that lifestyle. I was nine-years-old and I was beginning to make sense of my life, and understand the struggle that my parents and community had inflicted on me.

Drugs plagued me throughout my entire childhood, which made me look at all drugs in a negative way. I knew that I would never put my own children or myself in a situation like this. I didn't want to live with the negativity that stemmed from my parents' habits forever. I made a pact with myself that I would never use drugs, and to this day, I haven't.

Even though I didn't touch drugs, I must admit the neighborhood norms tempted me as well. My friends insisted that I join their gangs, and sell dope with them. They even wanted to go on drive-by shootings with them so that I could know what it felt like to kill someone. I must admit, I was curious to learn what it felt like to hang out with a group of my friends who were all doing the same thing together. I saw so many of them committing what appeared to be easy crimes, and I wanted to try it, too.

I wanted to take something from someone that was smaller than I was; I wanted to know what it felt like to have power over and respect from those who were younger than I; it was my turn to try a criminal lifestyle. I held back for so long. Why does it feel so good to them? Maybe I'm missing out on something. I figured I could use my young age to gain sympathy if I were caught, so I tried it. I approached a kid about my age and ripped a gold chain off his neck. He started crying and I started running as fast as I could because I didn't want anyone to figure out who I was and call the police. It was so easy; I knew I could go right down the street to the pawnshop and sell the chain for money. I was on my way there, when I was stopped by a group of guys who knew the boy with the chain, and they took it back from me. The guy I robbed had managed to find and tell his friends what had happened, and they ran down the street looking for me. I wish I had a gun. I want to shoot them for threatening me.

I was out-numbered, five-to-one, and it pissed me off. I figured the quickest way to defend myself would have been to shoot all of them. The only way I was able to get away from those guys was to tell them who my brothers were, and then they left me alone. Again, both of my brothers were in gangs, so I had their protection if things got rough for me. After that incident, I never again tried to hurt people in order to take something from them. The only things that I stole from then on were items that I could sneak from grocery stores or vending machines.

From small grocery stores like the 32nd Street market to the bigger college stores, my friends encouraged me to steal. At the time, I never looked at them or their actions as negative reinforcements, rather, I thought, my friends and I get what we want and we're having fun doing it. Eventually, it became more than just a means of survival; it grew to a point where we actually enjoyed the idea of the possibility of being caught.

If we were not stealing from a grocery store, we were breaking into the candy machines at the university. Eventually, the university figured out that my brothers and I were the ones breaking the candy machines and put a stop to that. They put bars over the glass of the candy machine, so that we couldn't reach the candy anymore. That didn't stop us; it just put "plan B" into action. We stole food from the local grocery store, and that went great until security caught us and had us arrested.

We were forced out of the store and our parents were called. No one was at my grandmother's house but my uncle, so he came down to the security station to pick us up. I was nervous because my uncle was the last person I wanted to pick me up. This was just another incident he could use as an excuse to discipline me. I was disappointed in myself because I had given him this opportunity. I had told myself that I would cut down on the stealing and go back to pumping gas. This ended my crime wave for the time being, and I started pumping gas and begging for money again. If there was money in the world to be earned, I was the young man who was going to earn it.

YOUR DISCIPLINE

You chastise me, but out of spite.
Instead of spanking me, you punch me, as if you want to fight.
I'm only nine years old,
But you are my guardian so I'll do as I'm told,
You don't have to beat me with your fist just because this is
your version or how to scold.
How cold, if you keep it up, I won't grow old.
I remember you pushing me on the dirt, kicking me while I
was down, you simpleton jerk
I hated your guts.
I prayed every night that God send somebody to come and kick
your butt.
You treated me like trash,
You smacked me upside my head. Only because I passed.
What did I ever do to you to deserve this treatment?
Couldn't you see that I was looking for somebody to talk to, so
I could vent,
But you were too immature to ask me why I did the things I
did.
You let your anger get the best of you, so you slapped a little
kid.
I hated the slum I was in
And I prayed to God to ask him why I couldn't be in a fami-
ly like Phil Drumin's.
I guess its different strokes for different folks, so I'm stuck here
with you,
Your discipline your anger and your can of brew.
You're not my dad, you know who brought this pain that's so
hard,
Yet this is your way of discipline, unaware that you've scared.

But it's cool, I'm grown and I prayed for this day for so long,
And now I am finally on my own
With my destiny in my hand.
Now I can learn from your mistakes and become a real man.
I wrote this, only with the intent to vent,
I needed to release my anger, so that I could circumvent.
With this release I end in peace.
Pain from the heart that now can cease.
To you, I write these words, now my skin is blue.

CHAPTER TWELVE

MY UNCLE AND HIS FAMILY MOVE IN

My uncle and his family moved into Grandmother's apartment like thieves in the night; no one knew they were coming. This took Grandmother by surprise the most; she was under the impression that my uncle and his family were doing fine. She couldn't turn them away because they had nowhere else to go, and she felt obligated to help them in there time of need, just as she had helped my mother in hers. This brought on a completely new set of problems. My uncle and his wife were still on drugs, therefore my grandmother had to hide the last of her expensive possessions, in fear that they would end up in a drug-dealers living room as payment. She was always worried about leaving my uncle, aunt, or mother in her house alone. She usually stayed home just to make sure they didn't have an opportunity to steal anything else.

Eventually, Grandmother was evicted because my uncle and his wife would not stop stealing from her, but she was able to maintain custody of my cousins because she didn't want them to face the consequences of their parents' mistakes. And what a high price it was when all the adults got together and smoked crack in my mother's apartment. At least I had a chance to spend some quality time with my cousin Winter.

During this time, an unfortunate event occurred. My cousin Winter was just four-years-old and she was an absolutely beautiful little girl. Her fair colored skin and green eyes made her look like a princess. One afternoon, Winter tried to follow Bernard across the street, and he had no idea she was following him. When he crossed it, Winter followed him and was hit by a car and drug approximately 50 feet down the street. She died instantly. When the driver finally stopped the car, he looked out the window at her body and popped open a beer and drank it. He didn't even get out of the car to check and see if she was all right. This was the first death in my own family that I had to experience, and I had no idea of how to respond to it. For the first time in my life, I realized that someone I truly cared about could be taken from me in an instant. I was ten-years-old and had no idea how much life meant until I lost my cousin.

My family responded with anger, and I remember them arguing over whose fault it was. I wondered, how selfish and shallow can they be? A little girl had just died. They were so caught up in blaming one another they didn't even take a moment to mourn for the loss of an innocent child's life and they continued to argue about how we were going to pay for the funeral. We didn't have much money, needless to say, so we walked house-to-house begging for money to pay for Winter's funeral. I was more than willing to go to every house in my neighborhood and ask for money so that my family could pay for the funeral. We started asking people for money early in the morning and continued until late in the day. It was the best thing that I thought I could ever do for Winter because she meant so much to me. We were able to raise enough money to give her the funeral she deserved, and it was a blessing from God that we were able to raise as much as we did.

After the funeral, all I could do was reminisce on all the good times I had with Winter. I walked up to my father and started crying in his arms because I missed my beautiful cousin so much When we got home, I remember my mother playing a song by Dianna Ross called *Missing You* and it made us all burst into tears. But the togetherness didn't last. My parents picked up where they left off with their drug use.

My grandmother never let the accident go; it stayed with her forever. Unfortunately, my uncle and his wife still used drugs. Not even the death of their own child could convince them to put down the pipe. They continuously brought problems into Grandmother's house, and they still didn't appreciate the blessing she was. She gave us shelter when we had none, she gave us food when our stomachs rumbled, she gave us love, and for that, she was rewarded with constant grief from my parents.

They constantly asked her for things she didn't have. When my mother needed to be bailed out of jail because she had been caught selling drugs, my grandmother used her entire savings to post her bail. When my uncle needed a co-signer for his car so that he could take his kids to and from the doctor's office, my grandmother co-signed. Now, what did they do for her in return? They did nothing but bring pain and misery into her life! Gradually it overwhelmed her and she was fed up with all their antics. She had arthritis throughout her body, which limited her from walking on her own, and she raised her grandchildren until she died.

Eventually, Grandmother became so weak that we had to help her with everything she did, and our parents couldn't care less. She welcomed eight kids in her three-bedroom apartment, and was never appreciated for it. My aunt, uncle, and mother still stole money from her, cursed at her, and tried to make her feel bad because she didn't want to support their drug habit. We watched her unfold, as the weight of our family slowly killed her.

My parents' behavior made our life with Grandmother miserable, and when the holidays came around things seemed to get even worse. Christmas was grim with silence and frowns. Grandmother would do her best to fix us up a great Christmas dinner. I remember pumping gas so that I could buy a toy to wrap and put it under the tree so that I would have something to open on Christmas morning. Even though I knew what it was, it still excited me on Christmas day, and I had something new to play with. My brothers laughed at me; they thought it was strange, but that did not bother me at all. I still had fun and valued the time I had with my new toy.

We went to a few places where they gave free toys to kids whose families couldn't afford Christmas gifts, and we got to ask Santa for some of the things we wanted, and he would give us the closest thing to it he could. Even if it wasn't exactly what we wanted, it was something, and we had fun with our new presents. We never knew what to expect for Christmas, but we never expected very much. What's funny is that to this very day, I have a hard time if anyone makes a big deal for me on Christmas or my birthday. It embarrasses me to no end because that's just something we never did or could do.

In all my years with my mother, we had one great Christmas that I can remember. There were presents everywhere and for one day, we had a drug-free family. My brothers and I stayed up for hours playing with our new toys and trying on our new clothes, but even our drug-free day wouldn't end in happiness. Eventually, all of our clothes were sold for drugs, but at least they left the toys for us to play with. It was a great Christmas, but drugs always had a way of creeping into the picture. It was something we could never escape from, so we learned to expect it and avoid its wrath by keeping our distance. Despite our attempts, misfortune always came back to haunt us.

    There were times when my aunt, uncle, and mother would steal the welfare checks that were delivered to my grandmother's house before she could get to them. That always left all of us in a hole, and it was every person for himself when it came to finding food. In order to keep the store clerk from getting suspicious, I would use some of the money I made at the gas station to buy something. When I bought an item, the owners didn't realize that we were stealing. By this time, I had become the ringleader of our schemes.

    My cousins and I made an agreement that if anyone got caught, we would discipline them so that the store clerk wouldn't call the police, or our parents. If that plan didn't work, then we would all run. My idea worked perfectly, and when we felt that we had hit a particular store too often we would relocate to another grocery store and do the same thing. Hey, desperate times led to desperate measures if we wanted to survive! We knew that it was wrong, but what other alternatives did we have? Our biological needs took control over all our decision-making ability, and we were all under the age of ten. We were too young and ignorant to understand the repercussions it could have had on our lives. We did what we had to in order to eat; the gas station couldn't feed everyone.

Our parents were running grandmother down and we could see the stress wearing on her. Even though we were young and immature, it didn't take much to realize our life was cruel and unkind. We watched as Grandmother's beauty faded away. She could no longer bear the weight of her children's addictions, responsibilities and mistakes. She became very weak and contracted cancer. I watched as my grandmother's life slowly slipped away everyday right before my eyes. I can't explain the pain I felt when she was too weak to walk with a cane, and the resentment I felt towards my mother who didn't seem to care. She just continued running the streets and using drugs, just like my uncle. When he and his family moved out, they didn't even bother coming back to see how Grandmother was doing. They maybe stopped by every once in a while, but not often to show her that they cared.

She became so sick we had to buy a bed for her so that she could be in the living room all the time. That way she didn't have to be carried back and forth to her bed, out of which she often rolled and hurt herself. Her new bed was specially sent from the hospital to help secure her at night so that she would be safe from falling out of her bed in her sleep. Helpless and practically abandoned, you could see the pain in her eyes. I spent hours crying because there was nothing I could do to help her. She had been my savior; the one who had repeatedly saved my brothers and me from the depths of hunger. My older brother was in juvenile hall, and the second to the oldest was gangbanging and robbing people to survive; Grandmother could no longer provide for us. She would be for gone days at a time and then show up, take the check, and try to tell us how to take care of Grandmother. Some people have all the nerve in the world, don't they? Anyway, we had to change Grandmother's diapers because she had no control over her bowels; she was helpless and longing to escape from the hell in which she lived.

Late one night I as I watched television with a friend, I was mad that we had nothing to eat in the house. The night before my brother and his friends had robbed someone and had a huge bag of food they were eating from, "feasting off their rewards," if you will. I remember asking, "How did you get all that food?"

He told me, "We robbed some people and went and bought it." The following night, my friend and I agreed to do the same. I left Grandmother's and headed towards a local nightclub that was located on the corner of our street. We spotted a man getting off the bus and figured that he had just been paid because it was Friday. As we approached him, we noticed another man across the street watching us, but we thought we were bad because we both had butcher's knives, so we gave him the finger and continued on our quest. The man who we had targeted to rob turned the corner and started running. We chased him, screaming, "Give us your money!" Unfortunately, we couldn't catch him. We stopped running to catch our breath, and decided to try it again on someone else.

As we turned to head back to the corner, we noticed the guy we flipped off coming our way. We continued heading towards him, but to our surprise, he started shooting at us. We turned and ran, ducking behind cars as the bullets ricocheted all around us. We could hear them passing by, and we were so terrified. We ran behind an apartment building, making a complete circle around them where we found a thick bush to hide behind. We listened as the guy looked around and asked a passersby, "Have you seen two kids come through here?"

We stayed in those bushes for at least an hour. When we finally built up enough courage to come out from behind the bush, we sprinted the entire way home. Faced with the same hunger we had left with, we tried to make do with the scraps we could find. Grandmother still lie motionless in her bed with a tear in her eye that I will never forget.

Grandmother's sickness finally got the best of her body and she had to be sent to the hospital. She lied there for two days before God called on her soul. It was about 11:30 p.m., and Bernard and I were listening to a song called Happy by The Boys. My mother received the phone call that Grandmother had passed away. She burst into our room screaming and crying uncontrollably, Bernard and I looked at each other in sadness and wept together on the end of the bed. The song continued to play and we tried to comfort each other because we knew that the Lord had taken our grandmother away from us and that she had to be happier with Him than she was on earth.

My mother ran out of the house hysterically screaming at the top of her lungs, crying out to Grandmother. We ran out after her, and as we came out of the house, our Bible club teacher came out of his house; he knew that my grandmother had been sick and had a suspicion that she had died. He scooped my mother into his arms and tried to comfort her as she lay in the middle of the street crying. That was a night of bittersweet sorrow, and all I wanted to do was to fall asleep and block out all the pain. As I fell into a deep sleep, I had a dream that same night that Grandmother did not die. I dreamt that she and I were at her house, and she was sitting in her chair and I on the couch. I said to her, Grandma I knew you were not dead, and she answered, My baby, what would make you think something like that. YOU know your grandma wouldn't leave you alone. I hugged her so tightly in my dream, afraid she would escape my clutches. When reality finally caught up with me, it broke my heart even more. I woke up and realized that Grandmother really was dead, and I burst into tears again. I woke Bernard so I could tell him about my dream. I think it scared him at first, but then he mourned with me.

Grandmother had been the world to us. She was the one who saved us from being split up and sent to foster homes. She was the one who gave us a better life; a better chance at being happy. Although she was probably one of the meanest old ladies in the world, she still gave her heart and home to her grandchildren. She was far from a pushover; she told you how she felt and didn't care what you thought of her afterwards, but we loved her for it because she was being real. Grandmother was the one we could always depend on to be there for us.

When she left me in the dark that night, I felt like my life could only get worse from now on. I could only wait for the turmoil that would inevitably unfold. In the back of my mind, I constantly prayed to get older so that I could escape the madness that surrounded me in my childhood. At times, I couldn't bear the reality of missing the only person who had truly cared about us. It haunted me daily and all I could do was try to come to terms with the fact that Grandmother was gone. Bernard and I continued living in her house, while Travie went off to stay with my cousins in Compton, California.

My mother and uncle tried to figure out a way to pay for Grandmother's funeral, but they just became agitated with each other and had huge arguments about the issue, which never seemed to resolve the problem. They both continued using drugs, and they delayed Grandmother's funeral for three weeks. My mom rarely came home; all she did was roam the streets looking for some dope to smoke. She would come home high and would not say a word to us. The only thing she might say was, "Did the check come in the mail?" I thought, How can I respect her? The amount of hatred I felt towards her accumulated. Finally, I lost the last ounce of respect for her that I might have had when she disrespected Grandmother's death by bringing a new man into my grandmother's house.

I remember I was awake when she got home. My brother and I were sitting in our room with the door closed, listening to music. I heard her come through the door and we pretended to be asleep. She came into the room and checked on us, then immediately shut the door. We shot up from the bed and about five minutes later, we heard her moaning in Grandmother's room next door. We couldn't believe that she was having sex in Grandmother's bed before we had even given Grandmother her final resting place. I have never forgiven my mother for doing such a demeaning act. I couldn't sleep that entire night, and when the morning rolled around, I went to see if my mother was asleep. To my disgust, there laid my mother and that man still asleep. I slammed the bedroom door and ran out of the house, on my way to school then. I didn't come home until late that night because I knew that my mother would not be there. She always walked the streets at night and got high with her drug friends. She would sleep the whole day and smoke the whole night.

When I got home, Bernard was looking at some pictures of Grandmother. I couldn't help but notice the sad look on his face. It was like he needed someone there to comfort him, and our mother was nowhere to be found. The day of my grandmother's funeral finally arrived. It was only the second funeral that I had ever been to, and it hit me like a ton of bricks. It was a beautiful funeral, even though Grandmother looked like she was made of plastic. She looked like someone else and it threw me for a second. I felt as if the woman I saw lying there was an impostor, but as I looked at the features of her hand, it brought back memories that I'll never forget. I remembered how wonderful she had been. I could now rest at ease, knowing that she would be resting in peace in heaven, soaring over the clouds and watching over her grandkids. I could finally say goodbye and, "I'll meet you at the crossroads."

The funeral was over, but we never drove to the burial site to watch her being buried. My mother broke the shocking news to the family; we were going to have her cremated. I had no idea that she was going to be cremated, and in my mind, it was wrong. My mother explained that we didn't have enough money to pay for the funeral plot, so she cremated her. She had enough money for drugs, but not enough for the burial of her own mother. It's amazing what kind of person crack can turn you into. For a long time, I couldn't believe that my mother had done something like that, after everything Grandmother had done for us. My mother carried the ashes with her every time we moved, but to this day, I have no clue as to where they are.

We continued living in Grandmother's house and my mother continued using drugs. It wasn't long, however, before my mother's neglect in paying rent caught up with her, and they evicted us. The U.S. Marshal came to the house and told us that we had two days to make sure we took all of our remaining furniture and clothes out of the house, and we were not allowed back on the premises. It amazed me because the officer came so early in the morning to serve us the papers. My mother knew that it was going to happen, so she was not surprised when the Marshal showed up at the front door. As soon as the officer left, my mother ordered Bernard and me to pack up our belongings, and said that she would be back later on that day. She didn't show up until the next morning; once again she had been smoking dope. When she got home, she was high and went straight to her room and closed the door. We continued packing and asking each other where were we going to live. We were both puzzled because my mother had not said anything to us about what we were going to do. Finally, later on that day, Mama woke up and told us that we were going to live in Compton with our cousin Jeanie. Jeanie had seven kids of her own and my brother Travie. They lived in a four-bedroom apartment, and we were about to add three more people to share those cramped quarters.

My uncle's kids had to go to a foster home because another one of their kids had died. She was running around in the house and slipped on the floor. She suffered severe brain damage, causing her death. Because her parents were on drugs, the county felt that they were not fit to raise children, so they took them away. My cousins were the only other family I really knew, and now they weren't around anymore either.

My cousins had gone through pretty much the same lifestyle my brothers and I had. Both of their parents were on drugs as well; they were more like our brothers and sisters than cousins. Seeing them in foster homes still weighs heavily on my heart; they were separated and lived in different locations. I couldn't imagine being separated from my brothers at such a young age and not having the ability to see them whenever I chose. It would have devastated me. I felt helpless; they didn't deserve to be broken up like that. I only wished I were older, so that I could adopt them and have them live with me, but I could only try to see them as much as possible. Their mother went to jail because the courts found her guilty of child neglect. She spent a year in jail before she could even attempt to win her kids back. All I could do was hope that, in the end, being in a foster home would be more beneficial than harmful to them. I hoped that they had more chances to accomplish their dreams. My brothers and I, on the other hand, had a different obstacle to overcome, and it was in Compton.

KEEPING ME DOWN

You shut me out from the mainstream
Limiting my direction, by placing a dam in the middle of my
stream.
You blind me by placing me in the confounds of the inner city
Shackling me in poverty, while others pity.
You deliver to my mind the inequalities of education
A lockout that confines me from liberation.
How bold is your heart?
It appears to be made of stone because this plan was devised
from the start.
You keep me down with drugs, poverty, and gangs
A manifested whole, which to the outsider may seem strange.
You keep me down by destroying my vision,
Killing my pride with this poverty living.
You let me float only within the barriers of the 'hood
You've bestowed upon me ills, and placed me in the center of
the woods.
You've blinded me; shut me out with façade's, better yet falla-
cies,
Which has resulted in this ghetto like mentality.
I am lost in this world,
I feel hopeless, and I think I am about to hurl.
Somebody please come save me from this pain,
It hurts so bad, I can't stand this constant black rain.
Someone come release me from this onslaught of hunger and
tears,
Someone please come dry up my tears.
All I ask is for someone to lift me from this fire
Because it is killing my chances to aspire.
Euthanasia is closing in fast
I can't take this rotten mess, Lord just let me pass
Take me to that place where you reside,

So that I can leave this place aside.
I pray that someone hears my plea
Because one more day on this earth I do not want to be.
If you can grant me this one wish, eternally I'll be grateful
Because the majority of the people I have seen are hateful,
May my cry be heard.

CHAPTER THIRTEEN

COMPTON

We moved into our cousin Jeanie's apartment and immediately the different personalities clashed. Jeanie, my mother's sister, was a large woman who wanted to feel empowered. She was my mother's relative, but she did speak with my father from time to time. Her moodiness made her impossible to live with, the worst of anyone I ever met. She had no clue how to run a household and took her frustrations out on her kids. Her tall and big boned figure established her control over everyone who lived under her roof, and she loved it. Jeanie was the type of person who would beat her kids until she saw blood. I hated living with her! She filled the house with negativity and animosity every day.

The house was always filthy. Occasionally Jeanie would get in one of her moods and make everyone clean up, but our personal hygiene was horrible. We only showered, maybe, twice a week. Being twelve years old and as active as I was, I should have been showering twice a day, but it was not encouraged in our house, so no one ever did. The women living in Jeanie's house used socks as tampons, and then threw them in the bathroom trashcan for everyone to see. With no end to the filth, it was disgusting! Everyone in that house went through life without a purpose and ignored all biological/health concerns. As long as we stayed out of Jeanie's way, we could avoid conflict.

The adults in the house did not like each other, and flashed fake smiles when they crossed paths. My mom would talk poorly about Jeanie, and Jeanie would say the same about my mom. As kids, we would always tell each other what one adult said about the other. To avoid fights, the parents really did not interact unless they shared a mutual feeling on a given topic. Living there was like walking on eggshells. You had to do your best to make sure you didn't piss-off the "landlord," or Jeanie would evict us in a second. She repeatedly threatened to kick us out whenever she had a bad day. Her attitude influenced me to get involved with extra-curricular activities after school.

I joined the football team as well as the track team. I also tried to get a job, so that I could make a little money. Everyone there was so lazy that they could suck the energy right out of you and made it easy to get caught up in their way of thinking. I refused to settle. That's the key to surviving the ghetto; refuse to settle for the crumbs put in front on you. Fight for something more!

My hunger grew as I matured, and no one could satisfy my cravings, but myself. I worked at a hamburger stand cleaning up at night. I was twelve so I was paid under the table. My family didn't even know I had a job until they came down to eat at the hamburger stand one day while I was working. It didn't shock them, though; they knew I liked to make money, so they sat down, ordered their food, and went on their merry way.

My life was stagnant for a while, but then my grandfather died exactly a year after Grandmother's death. This tragedy showed me how much more ignorant my mother and uncle were. My grandfather's death came unexpectedly; we had no idea he was even sick. We had never really spent time with him, but we still loved him dearly. He and my grandmother had been divorced and lived apart, so we spent most of our time with Grandmother. At the time of his death, my grandfather's house was up for sale and was in foreclosure. My mother and uncle inherited around $32,000 for the house. They divided it up between the two of them, and all hell broke loose. My mother gave my brothers and me around $700, then rented a limousine and took her boyfriend out on the town. They were both drug addicts and had one thing on their mind—getting high. They drove off in their limo and didn't come back for two weeks.

My mother had paid two months of Jeanie's rent, which equaled $2,000, and took the remaining money to have "fun." When she came back, she had nothing left but the clothes on her back. I could not believe she could spend that much money in that little amount of time. I was even more pissed at her because we could have used that money to move out of Jeanie's filthy house. We could have started all over toward a better life, but instead of looking out for her family, my mother looked out for her habit. This just fueled my fire. I was about to become an inferno. She spent over $12,000 and had nothing to show for it. My uncle blew his half of the money, too and was nowhere to be found. Worst of all, he didn't even give his kids any money. He could have put some money away in an account or tried to get them back, but instead he vanished and spent all of it.

When my mother came home two weeks later, things went on as if she hadn't inherited anything at all and Jeanie still had the upper hand in our lives. Even though my mother gave Jeanie $2,000, she still was bitter that she didn't get more.

She actually had the nerve to tell my mother, "You're cheap. I want $2,000 more because I deserve it." It didn't matter that my mother had paid her rent for the next two months; she still felt she deserved a bigger cut from my mother's money. They argued about it for weeks and finally Jeanie kicked us out of her apartment and we were forced to live in a motel.

When my mother received her welfare check, we moved into a hotel called Dalivarden. This was a six-story hotel in very poor condition located in downtown Long Beach. Sometimes, the water ran brown from the faycet, and we had roaches everywhere. We all lived in one small room and had no privacy at all. Bernard got a job at a local drugstore, so he was gone all the time. I continued to pump gas and begged for money. I was only thirteen. I commuted an hour and a half to school in Compton because it was too late in the semester to transfer. My mom got a job working at another local hotel cleaning rooms and occasionally working the front desk. We ultimately moved out of Dalivarden Hotel because my mother couldn't pay the rent, and we moved into the hotel where she worked because it was cheaper. Her rent was half the normal cost because the money she made there only covered half of the rent. This hotel room was a little bigger than the previous one we had stayed in, and Bernard and I would joke around and say we were moving up in the world because we had a kitchen. This arrangement was great until the plague of cocaine revisited my mother's life.

Up until then, she had been doing great; she wasn't doing drugs and she had even started going to church, but the devil got the best of her once again. She became hooked on her destroyer of life. She stayed out all night and came home in the morning, still high. At this point, I started selling baseball cards to my teacher for money. Business flourished, and in my eyes, I was progressing in life. Bernard was working also, so we didn't need our mother to buy us food anymore; we could do it ourselves. Travie was staying with my father's mother and my older brother, Peanut, was still incarcerated at a halfway house.

My mom frequently asked, "Eboni, Bernard, do you have any money?"

We always replied, "We don't have any," so she would turn around and leave. We hid our money on the top of the kitchen cabinet so that my mother wouldn't be able to steal it. Her drug habit made her do anything she had too in order to get her fix. One night she stole a gold ring that I had found right off my finger while I was sleeping. I am such a deep sleeper, so I didn't feel a thing. I was outraged but I never confronted her about it. Why? What more could you expect from an addict? Once I mentioned the situation to her to see what she would say.

"Mom, I lost my ring. Have you seen it?" I let the topic die with her wondering if I knew she had stolen it from me. She didn't confess to stealing the ring until years later, but the look in her eye when I brought it up, she told me that she had.

Bernard and I did everything we could to stay away from home. We would go to the mall for hours at a time, just so we didn't have to stay in that hellhole. I remember taking Bernard out to Sizzler for his sixteenth birthday and seeing the appreciation on his face. It was enough to lift my spirits for the rest of my life; we developed an extremely close relationship during this period.

One night my mother was out getting high, and I had a sneaking suspicion that she was going to search the house for our money when she returned. So I took my money from the top of the cabinet and hid it in my shoe. Bernard kept saying, "Don't do that. Mom is gonna find it."

"No, she won't." I said. I refused to listen to him and pushed my shoe as far as I could under the bed. I thought that there was no way she would be able to find it. I was not about to let her take my hard earned money away from me! I was the one who had pumped gas and sold baseball cards, not her. But lo and behold, I awoke the next morning with eighty-five cents left from one hundred and twenty dollars. She took all my money and smoked it away before I even woke up. My anger led to tears that scorched my face, and I went to school with no money and no way to eat. I remember Bernard telling me, "I told you so," but he let that go and comforted me in my bitterness.

As I composed myself and found the nerve to go to school even though I was broke, Bernard and I ran into my mother as we were walking out of the hotel room. I remember her saying, "I hate you!" Her reaction made me feel guilty, even though she was the one who was dead wrong. Her eyes flooded with tears and she said, "I am going to kill myself. Then you won't have to worry about me stealing from you anymore."

She went on to apologize. "I'm sorry I cause you all this pain." She went into our hotel room, grabbed a handful of pills, and swallowed them all. My brother and I rushed to stop her as she threw them into her mouth. Bernard grabbed the bottle from her, and I grabbed her throat so that she couldn't swallow the pills already in her mouth. Together we managed to make her spit out all the pills she had taken. She started to cry.

"Relax and lie down," we told her and we comforted her until she fell asleep. This is why I said she was a drama queen. If she couldn't lie to get out of it, she always flipped it around and made herself the victim. We did not go to school that day because we were worried that she would try to kill herself again. We both agreed that one of us would stay up at all times to make sure that she did not do anything to harm herself. She awoke the next day after not sleeping for three days.

My mother and I talked about what had happened. "Do you realize what happened last night? I love you, but you're killing yourself and your killing us, too."

She agreed that she would ease off the drugs. My mother woke up, fixed us breakfast and relaxed with us on that beautiful Saturday morning. The day was going well until the manager knocked on our door.

He said to my mom, "You're fired. You have to the end of the month to move out." She had apparently stolen money from the hotel office and had bought drugs with it. We had nowhere to go but back to Jeanie's house. We had to beg her to let us stay with her again.

We were back in our own private hell that we had escaped six months ago. The house was still dirty, and the kids still smelled as rancid as ever. Jeanie's attitude hadn't changed, but why should it? She enjoyed being the evil lady she was! In fact, the only reason that she let us stay with her was because she enjoyed having some kind of power or authority over people. She liked telling people what to do. She said, "Remember whose house you're in." I avoided all contact with her. She was the type of person who sucked all the positive energy from you. She had a poor attitude with everyone with whom she came into contact and raised her daughters to be dependent on her for everything.

Her children lived with her until they were in their mid-twenties because she had convinced them that they couldn't make it without her and that they were too stupid to make it on their own. She had told them that if they ever tried to leave and didn't make it, she wouldn't let them come back home. She depended on her kids for a purpose in life, so she broke them down and made them as weak as possible. She gave them whippings even when they were in their twenties. They didn't have enough nerve to tell her that they were too old to be getting spankings. She convinced them they needed her to survive, and that no one would care about them as much as she did. I've never seen a mother beat her children the way she did. She gave them black eyes, punched them in their guts and anywhere else she could reach.

My mother left us with Jeanie. She took off because she couldn't stand having to swallow her pride every time she walked into Jeanie's house. She left us behind because we didn't have anywhere else to stay. The only time we heard from my mother was when her checks came. She paid rent, gave my brothers and I twenty dollars, and left to go smoke up the rest of the money. Jeanie constantly told my brothers and me, "Your mother's worthless. She doesn't really care about you. If she did, she would try to get you your own house."

We knew that Jeanie was full of it. She never gave our mom an opportunity to save the little money we needed to move into our own apartment; she always demanded her rent. So we just listened when Jeanie ridiculed my mom and her habit and took it with a grain of salt. I could see changes somewhere deep in my mother's heart. I thought, if only Jeanie gave my mother a chance.

One night after work, Jeanie was in one of her moods and met me in the driveway of her apartment building. She was shouting, "Where the hell have you been?"

"I was working." This was something she already knew, but

refused to acknowledge it.

"You're a dumb a--, and you're worthless."

I knew I hadn't done anything wrong, but I kept my cool and acted nonchalant. "Okay, I agree with you."

That made her even angrier until she finally said, "You gotta quit your job. If you go back to that job, you'll leave my house."

I exploded in anger and rushed towards her, screaming at her, "I don't give a f--- what you say. I'm gonna to work anyway!" She was petrified as though I was going to hit her or something. Everyone grabbed me, including her boyfriend. He tried to manhandle me to show his authority, but this only infuriated me more.

"Get the hell out of my house and never come back."

I went into the house and packed my clothes. My brothers and cousins looked at me as though I was crazy and did not say one word to me. I had a trash bag full of clothes and I headed for the door when, out of nowhere, Jeanie pushed me into the bathroom and held a knife to my throat, screaming, "I'm gonna kill you!" She said, "I should kill your black a-- for rushing me like that."

I was so pissed that I told her to go right ahead and do it! I egged her on, "Go ahead, kill me. At least I won't have to live here no more! Kill me. I'd be better off anyway. I don't care if I die!"

She looked at me as if I was crazy. "Get the hell outta my house!"

Tears ran down my face because I knew I would not see my brothers for a while. I had been talking to Peanut, who was still in a juvenile halfway house. I visited him a few of times and it was about a four hour bus ride there. He lived in Canoga Park and attended a local high school. That's where I was headed and had every intention of staying in the halfway house with my brother, even if it meant having to listen to people tell me what to do and when to be in the home. It was late and raining the night that I started my journey. I wore dark glasses on the bus so people wouldn't be able to tell that I was asleep. It took longer to arrive at my destination because Canoga Park was flooded. I remember getting off the bus to find water flooding the bottom stair. I hopped over the curb and onto the sidewalk that was soaked. I finally reached the halfway house at about 3 a.m.

I slept in the Winchell's doughnut shop on the corner with my sunglasses on because I was afraid that someone would try to take my garbage bag full of clothes. When morning arrived, I went down the street to where my brother stayed, and I found the lady who looked after my brother.

"Could I stay here, too? I have nowhere else to go." I stated.

She asked, "Do you know where your father is?"

"No," I told her. I actually did know where he was and even knew his phone number, but I didn't want to stay with him because he was on drugs, too.

She then asked, "Do you want to stay in a foster home?"

I said, "No, why can't I stay here?"

"It's against the rules. You have to be placed in an institution like this." She proceeded to dial foster care and that scared me bad enough to confess.

"I know where my father is. I have his phone number." She was upset and curious as to why I had said I didn't know where he was, but she called him anyway.

My father was upset that I had gone to the juvenile detention center looking for a place to live and made me come and live with him in his hotel in Inglewood. He gave me directions, and the lady who worked at the detention home gave me bus tokens, and I was on my way. I couldn't help but feel scared because I didn't know what to expect from my father.

All I knew was that he had a history with drugs and would probably steal from me just like my mother had. I didn't know what I was getting into and I wondered, had I crawled into an even deeper hole than the one I was trying to escape? Should I have gone into the foster care that the lady at the detention center recommended? At least there I would have been assured warm meals and clothes. Or maybe the foster care facility would be unbearable, too. I feared what I didn't know. I was so scared that I refused to explore my options. At least I had some idea of what to expect with my father; I knew what kind of man he was. I was scared of foster care. What would they think of me? Would they reject me, or would they accept me and try to make my life better? All of these thoughts ran through my mind. I knew what it felt like to live in a hotel, but this time it was only me; Bernard was not there to share my sorrows.

The thought of not having anyone there to understand what I was going through made me wonder, should I get off the bus and head back to the juvenile center and try out a foster home? Maybe I should try this new uncharted world. I hate the one I'm living in. I probably would have been better off and free of sorrow, but I never worked up the nerve to get off the bus. Instead, I accepted my destiny and welcomed back the life I already knew. The closer I got to my destination, the more my heart raced. I even thought about living on the streets, where at least I wouldn't have to deal with my family. I knew that I could make enough money to eat. I even rang the bell to get off the bus to pursue this new life, but when I stepped off and looked at the sadness in the eyes of the bums who were outside, I quickly changed my mind. I actually found something worse than the life I was living and so I continued to my father's room, where he awaited my unwanted arrival. I knew that my father hadn't expected to have one of his sons live with him, but he would have felt more guilty if he had turned his back on me again. When I finally arrived, he welcomed me into his life.

Living with my father didn't last long. It was okay for a while; he gave me lunch money for school and always had food in his room. He even worked at a dry cleaner's where several of my family members had worked over the years. The job paid fairly well, and he seemed to be somewhat satisfied. Although everything appeared to be going smoothly, he was really just hiding his addiction very well.

I knew he had a drug habit, but he was never high in front of me and seemed to pay all the bills before he spent the remaining money on drugs. My father created a balance between drugs and responsibility. He kept this up for awhile, but then the drug use progressed and it took over as it had with my mother. The drugs soaked up his time and money. He came home high, if he came home at all. If he stayed out, he would come home the next day as if nothing had happened at all. I could tell that my time there was ending. The short, "normal" life that I seemed to be living was snuffed out like a candle in the wind.

One day Jeanie showed up at our motel when my father was out getting high; he had called her to come pick me up because he couldn't take care of me anymore. It surprised me to see her. It seemed like she was just in the neighborhood and had stopped by to see my father. Well I was wrong. She came over to take me to her house and I wondered, what did my dad do to convince her to let me stay there again? It must have been pity. When she arrived, my father was walking down the street, high on the drugs that he had just smoked.

She said, "Get your clothes and get in the car." I knew she was pissed at my father for being high; she didn't say a word to him. I got in the car and I was on my way back to the hellhole I thought I'd escaped. I didn't say one word to her on the way to her house, and she didn't say a word to me. I could tell that this would be another one of my unpleasant experiences in life; I had no control of where I lay my head or with whom I had to put up with in order to survive. I had to wait until I was of age to do the things I wanted to do to succeed. Until then, I had to endure the unfairness that faced me everyday. As we pulled into the driveway of her apartment, my heart fell to the ground because I knew what awaited me on the other side of that door.

Everything was just how it was when I left, dirty! Nothing had changed since then. My brothers were a welcomed sight, but my mother was more depressed than ever. It surprised me to see her there. She was probably out of money and couldn't afford any drugs. I did not want to be there, and I resented every moment that I was forced to be. I constantly contemplated running away. I couldn't take Jeanie's outbursts of pure hate; the only way I could escape her and the lunacy of her house was to go to school everyday.

I couldn't work at the hamburger stand anymore because Jeanie didn't approve of it, and my mother didn't take a stand for me because she wasn't there enough. So I had to improvise. I sold candy at my junior high school to make money for food. I went to a discount store where they sold candy in bulk, and took it to school to sell at a price where I could make a profit. Once the school figured out that I was selling candy without their permission, they threatened to suspend me if I didn't stop, but I didn't let that stop me. I just figured that I would deny that I sold candy if they tried to catch me. My business lasted until the students got bored with the same kind of candy every day.

Jeanie started asking questions. "Where did you get your money? Are you stealing from me boy?" How you can steal something that isn't there and isn't missing, is beyond me. I just went about my business and tried to ignore her. I created a spot to hide my money because everyone knew I had some. They tried to steal it from me when I was asleep. They knew I was a hard sleeper so they would search my pants for money at night, but I had a secret hiding place—a small hole in the wall of the closet. I also had some money hidden in a small slit in the carpet in a corner in the room. I always made sure that no one saw me when I stashed my money; that way I could be sure that it would be there when I woke up the next morning. It was a shame that I had to go through so much to hide my money from all of the adults I knew.

Finally, God answered my prayers and helped us get out of Jeanie's house. My mom had some friends who managed apartments in Long Beach. They offered to help her move into an apartment if she helped to clean up around the premises. This was our ticket out, and to my surprise, our mother accepted the offer. We told Jeanie, "We are moving out!" We were going to be in our own apartment, and she couldn't do anything to stop us.

HEAVY RAIN

As the heavy rain falls on the ghettos where we lay
It camouflages our tears that cause our pride to be washed
away.
And as the pain run down our face
Saturating our life with injustices, feeling disgraced,
We rise like the sun
Full of grace with ultimate precision.
Blessed with our majestic essence, which is the root of our soul
Giving us the wisdom to see through the fallacies, which are
hidden in the coal.
Our existence is sacred
Yet the heavy rain tries to drown us, so that we don't make it.
Our destiny was determined by a hateful decision,
The heavy rain came and destroyed our vision.
It washed us away from our warm sweet land
On too this uncharted, cold, deserted island.
We were washed ashore, away from our home
Forced to survive, all alone.
Yet we rose
Like the hidden sun beyond these dark clouds,
We fought with determination, black and proud.
Yet the hard rains only got heavier,
Limiting us to push further.
What are we to do in this unfamiliar wilderness filled with
bitterness?
Where the cold hard rain is horrendous,
It pierced our backs and left us with bloody cracks.
Heavy rain why do you hunt for blacks?
You drowned our leaders,
Tried to break our pride and even washed away the food that
fed us.
Education,

*You knew that if we were denied food of knowledge it would
limit our chances of liberation.*

Why?

*We didn't ask to be washed on these cold lands
You stole us and we were forced to heed your demands.
We picked your cotton, and plucked your fruit.
You even made us get down on our knees and shine boots.
We built your buildings from our blood, sweat, and tears,
But you continued to rain harder cause it was us you feared.
Dark rain please go
So that we can build and grow.
We don't ask to take your place
We demand to walk the same pace.
We are tired of driving you around, entertaining you kids by
playing the clown;
We are tired of washing your clothes, and seeing you use our
women for hoes.
All we ask is to co-exist
We don't ask to take over and put you in the same position as
this.
We know how the pain feels,
We just want an equal chance so that we can provide our fam-
ily with warm meals.
And a cozy place to stay
Cause on that cold concrete, another day I will not lay.
The revolution has begun,
Full speed ahead and already won.
The heavy rain will soon go afar,
And on that day the sun will rise as the greatest star
And will be as one.*

CHAPTER FOURTEEN

OUT OF THE FRYING PAN AND INTO THE FIRE

Bernard, mother, and I moved into a one-bedroom apartment. My little brother stayed with Jeanie. He liked the elementary school he was attending, and he wanted to graduate from it. I never did understand why my mother let him stay with Jeanie. It bothered me a lot, but I think my mom thought it would be easier to take care of two kids, rather than three. I can honestly say that after the age of fourteen, my mother no longer took care of my older brother, Peanut, the jail system did.

Being in and out of jail so often, Peanut actually seemed to enjoy being in jail more than being out. Bernard and I, on the other hand, still worried about where we would find our next meal. When we moved into our new apartment, our lives were supposed to turn around, but that promise was quickly broken.

The manager who let us stay in the apartment was kind. He and his wife were recovering drug addicts who were trying to do well for their two kids. Bernard and I always went over to their house because they always had food. They made us breakfast, lunch and dinner, even snacks in between. My mother said, "It's rude to pop-in at other people's houses just for food. Stop going over there so much." Like we had any other choice! This only made us mad because my lazy mother rarely looked for a job to change our living conditions. She would rather sit around the house all day and wait for the mailman to come so that she could collect her welfare check. It was heartbreaking and I refused to sit at home and watch my mother's life wither away, with no meaning, so I started going to the gym across the street. That's where I started taking out all my frustrations that built up from the day.

Living in Long Beach right across the street from a park and a gym really helped me reflect on what was going on in my life. I was never home because I always needed to escape the reality of my hell. It was enough to drive me to suicidal thoughts—thoughts I dared not explore. I went to the park and reflected on my mother's dependence on drugs, and how my father really wanted to help us but his dependencies misguided him. Then I went to the gym and lifted for three hours, just because I needed that release that I couldn't explain to anyone. I felt like no one understood what I went through anyway, so what was the point of talking to someone?

After working out I pumped gas again so that I could afford to buy some food. Once again, I tried to avoid going home at all costs. The good thing about my new living arrangements was that I never had to worry about Jeanie's mood swings. Even if I had to travel more than an hour to go to school, I didn't care. It gave me peace of mind not to have to deal with anyone for an hour-and-a-half. It worked out great and helped me to find some inner peace. To me, living in the one bedroom apartment was better than living in Compton, even if it wasn't an ideal living arrangement, but

Bernard soon left and went back to live with Jeanie.

Bernard was fed up with my mother and her drugs, and wanted to go back to live with Jeanie because his gang friends lived in that neighborhood. He wanted to go back to his gang who shared his mutual feelings and mutual circumstances in life. When Bernard left, the situation with my mother got worse. She started leaving me alone in the apartment for days at a time so that she could go get high in L.A. somewhere. She would come back just to show her face and then leave again. I no longer had my brothers in my life and my mother was in L.A. with my father, smoking crack and giving up on hope. My life began to slide backwards, deeper into poverty's pit. Eventually, my mother stopped coming home at all. She just stayed away and smoked dope all the time. I had to sell baseball cards to my teacher to make money to eat; I had told my teacher about my situation, so he bought baseball cards from me even if he didn't want them. I could tell he really cared about me and wanted to see me succeed. He did everything in his power to educate me, so that I would not be trapped in the ghetto.

His name was Mr. Coleman. Without him, I would have gone hungry a lot more often than I had. He always encouraged me not to give up on life just because of what my parents were doing; he saw promise in me and I saw promise in that. Even though my mother left me alone in that apartment with no food for three months, I did not give up on myself because he wouldn't give up on me.

I liked being on my own; I didn't have to deal with my mother and her fixes or late night raids on any money I had. I liked how quiet the house was. I could live in peace. Even though I struggled to find food, I was willing to pay that price. At one point, I called my father to tell him that my mother had left me at the apartment by myself, and he was furious. He told me that I should wait for a while to see if my mother was going to come back. After a month passed and there was no sign of Mama, I dealt with the fact that they didn't really care about me or else one of them would have come to my aid. My father may have felt sorry for me, but he didn't want to offer me his room. Two months passed and the only time I saw my mother was when she carne to pick up the welfare check. She said she was going to go cash the check, and come back to give me some money, but she never did. This only opened my eyes even more to what she was capable of, and I could see what was really important to her. So I continued fending for myself, and didn't think twice about it. I had to survive.

I would go directly to the gas station after school and start working. If business wasn't going well there, I would beg for money, and if that didn't work I would steal the food I needed. I was desperate and the only way I knew how to survive was by hustling. Sometimes my friends would give me the baseball cards that were only worth a nickel, and I would turn around and sell them to my teacher for a few dollars, who probably knew their worth, but just wanted to help me out. I did what I had to do to survive, and yet the black rain still came crashing down on my life.

Three months had passed and still no sign of my mother to me help me out. The manager had posted an eviction notice on our door and said we had until the end of the month to move out. Apparently my mother had not been paying the rent, and because we knew the manager, he had prolonged our eviction. I told my father that we were being evicted, and he offered to share his room with me once again, but this time, I refused. I knew what I was getting into if I went to go live with him again, so I stayed where I was. Finally, my mother came back home and brought my uncle and his family with her. He had three kids at the time, and all hell was about to break loose, again.

It appeared that my mother had been living close to my uncle. He and his wife had been smoking dope with her. They were all taking the money they received from the government and buying drugs. This went on for three months before my uncle was finally evicted from his house. When the rent was due and he refused to pay, the repercussions were prompt.

There were now seven people in a one-bedroom apartment with another on the way, my aunt was nine months pregnant. Even though she was pregnant, she continued using drugs. One night my mother woke me up and told me that my auntie was having her baby. It occurred to me that my aunt, mother and uncle were all getting high that night. I woke up and saw my aunt sitting on the toilet with her new-born baby. The baby was born high on drugs; her mother had just finished smoking a half-hour earlier. It was crazy because my aunt was so high that she hadn't felt any pain while giving birth. The baby came right out without her even having to push. I believe it was a gift from God that the baby didn't have to suffer any longer. It was the saddest thing I had ever seen, her getting high while she was pregnant.

I was at the age where I understood that whatever my aunt did; she did it to the baby as well. I was fourteen-years-old, and I felt like I was twenty-five. I was very observant, and I watched as my aunt destroyed the brain cells of an innocent child. It was hard for me to witness the things that went on in my life, but I had to because it was my life. The ambulance came and my aunt tried to cover the fact that she had been getting high, and the paramedics never asked.

I'm fed up living through this. I want to run away. I knew a day would come when all the adults would leave the house, so I waited patiently. In the meantime, I had asked my mom if could I go and live with my father, but she refused. I had been on my own for three months and it was strange listening to my mother tell me what I could and could not do. This only fueled my rage even more, but the day finally came that I could escape the hellhole in which I lived.

My mother, uncle and his family had all left to beg for money in a nearby wealthy neighborhood. They took the kids because it brought more sympathy when they went door to door asking for it. They even had the audacity to take the newborn baby that should not have been outside in the first place. The moment they left, I went to the manager's house and called my father.

"I'm coming to live with you." I told him that I was coming to live with him, and he said it was okay. I went back to our apartment, packed my bags and hopped on the bus. I was so happy to get out of that house; I knew it would still be rough living with my father, but it was better than living with my mother. I was on my way to the motel again and I knew that my father was probably still on drugs, but I didn't care. My mother was going to be irate when she saw that I wasn't at home, but I didn't care. There was nothing that was going to stop me from going to live with my father. I now left her set of problems behind and welcomed the totally new set of problems that came from living with my father. What was I supposed to do when poverty and drugs haunted me wherever I went?

There I was living in my father's motel room, commuting back and forth to school and doing whatever it took to survive in a family where drugs and poverty dictated our lives. I commuted from Inglewood to Long Beach to attend Long Beach Jordan High School. Back in my father's room, it felt like I had never left.

Benny still did his drug thing, and I continued to avoid him when he was high. The good thing about living with my father was that he cooked dinner for me, and he always kept food in the fridge, but the drugs were always there as well. I still couldn't trust him. It was hard for me to trust anybody for that matter; everybody except my grandmother had tried to steal whatever valuables I had. Inevitably, I became very suspicious of everything that went on around me, and those types of feelings towards my father only put our living situation on edge. I hid everything that meant something to me because I didn't want him to steal it, but my time in my new home with my father was coming to an end. Despite all his short-comings, I still appreciated him letting me live with him.

I began to hang around with an older kid named Laron. He and I were like two peas in a pod; we were inseparable. Laron wanted to be in a gang, so he acted like he was from a Blood gang in San Diego. He would dress in all red and act the part of someone who was affiliated with a gang. We probably clicked so quickly because my family was centered around the Bloods, so we shared a common bond. He was in eleventh grade and I was in the ninth. Although he was actually older than me, people always thought I was older than him because I was physically bigger, and that made it easy for us to hang out. We hung out a lot, and he influenced me in committing my first felony.

One Saturday, Laron and I were bored and he brought up

the idea of stealing a car. At this point in my life, I didn't care about myself or what I did, so I jumped at the idea and off we went. I had never even driven before and I was curious about how to do it. We ended up at a local sweatshop in downtown Los Angeles where the employees were working the graveyard shift. We entered the parking lot. Both of us were very nervous, but that only added excitement to our endeavor. Laron then showed me how to break the steering-wheel column and snap the pin that started the car, and we were off! It was that easy.

We just drove around town looking for girls. It was an exciting moment for me. I was already looking forward to the next car we could steal. After our tour of L.A., I had to go back to Inglewood and the motel room I shared with my father. I wanted to keep the car we stole, so I could drive it to school the next day, but Laron wanted to go back to Long Beach, so we looked for another car to steal so that he could get home that night.

We found a victim vehicle that Laron wanted and pulled up along side of it. The excitement started allover again. This time I broke the steering-wheel column and started up the car to see if I really knew what I was doing. The most daring thing about this theft was that the car we stole was directly across the parking lot from the room my father stayed in. If he had just looked outside of his window, he would have seen us breaking into a car, but that didn't bother me. I continued doing what I was doing - grand theft auto. Once the car was started, Laron climbed in and took off for home so he could make his curfew, and I went inside like nothing had happened.

I was so anxious to drive to school the next day that I could hardly sleep. Laron didn't let me drive when we first stole the car because he was scared that I would kill him. He had driven the whole time but it would finally be my turn in the morning. That night I asked my father all types of questions about how to drive a car to make sure that I knew what I was doing so that I wouldn't get pulled over by the police for driving out of control. I asked him every question I could think of because I was excited, but also very nervous. He had no clue I was asking him these questions because I had a stolen car waiting for me outside. He answered me in as much detail as possible, and every time he answered, I felt that much closer to driving. I finally forced myself to go to sleep; I figured the faster I went to sleep, the faster I would get into my new car. My father and I woke up around the same time. He had to be at work early in the morning, but I left thirty minutes before he did, which was good because this gave me time to get into the car before he came outside. I knew that he sometimes looked outside when I left, so I pretended that I was going to the bus stop. When I knew that he was not looking anymore, I ran to the car, started it up, and ducked low to the ground so that he couldn't see me and off to school I went. This was the beginning of another one of my impulse decisions, and ultimately, it was a mistake.

When I got into the car and started on my way to school, I had no clue what was in store for me. I was nervous behind the wheel because I had no real clue how to drive a car. All I knew was what I had seen Laron do and what my father had told me the night before. The car windows were fogged up because I hadn't given the car time to warm up. I couldn't see so I had to roll down my window to have some kind of visibility. Eventually, I had to pull over, but I wasn't worried because I was out of my father's sight and had plenty of time to let the windows defrost. Finally, I was off again and my vision was clear. I thought, I'm the man! I had never driven before, but I became comfortable behind the wheel right away.

Therefore, it was time to blast the radio. I was in my own world.

Despite the window being busted out in the back, I still managed to look inconspicuous because I had rolled down all of the windows to match the broken one. I was so engulfed in my own world that I didn't notice the police lights flashing in my rear view mirror; the music was so loud that I didn't hear the siren or the cop telling me to pull over on the loud speaker. I was on a mission and no one could stop me, but my joy ride ended when a motorcycle cop pulled in front of me and directed me to pull over to the side of the road.

My heart jumped into my throat. Part of me wanted to run and another part wanted to pullover. If I had not seen the police car behind me, I might have tried to run from the motorcycle cop, but to my misfortune, at least four cop cars surrounded me. The cops ordered me out of the car and on my knees; their guns were drawn and pointed at me as though I was on the Americas Most Wanted list. I was horrified and regretted not running away when I had the chance.

I was handcuffed with my face pressed on the concrete, and then the questioning began. "What's your name?" "Where did you get this car?" "Who was with you when you stole the car?" "Where were you going?"

I was bombarded with so many questions I had no idea which one to answer first.

"How old are you?"

"I'm fourteen." They all laughed because they didn't believe me; my size was deceiving.

"You should be playing football somewhere, not stealing cars. How the hell did you get so big? Why are you up so early in the morning?"

"I live two hours from school and I was headed there." After all their questioning, they picked me up off my knees, put me into a police car, and took me to the precinct.

I was a minor so they called my father and told him to come and pick me up from jail. I asked the cops, "Could you place me in a foster home?" I was afraid of what would be done to me. At the very least, he was going to beat the hell out of me, and I didn't want to face him. They told me no, so there I was, in jail, waiting for my father to pick me up. I was scared because I knew my father was going to be livid. I was trying to think of ways I could run away from him when we got outside the precinct house. I figured that was my best chance to get away. He wouldn't beat me in from of the cops, and if I darted away right when we got out of the precinct, I might have a chance of seeing my next birthday.

When he finally arrived, I could see the disgust in his face. He kept repeating to me, "I don't believe you played me like that. Askin' me all those questions about driving and then going out and stealing a car." He said, "I was wondering why you were askin' me all those questions, but I didn't really give it a second thought."

When we went outside, he just kept talking to himself and became so pissed off that he reached over to hit me, but then realized where we were and backed off. I thought I was going to get an a---kicking right in front of the police station. My aunt was outside waiting for us because she had given my father a ride. She took me back to the hotel and my father back to work. I had to stay in the room until my father came home. I was wondering what he was going to do when he finally got me alone, but to my surprise he didn't hit me. He just grounded me and yelled at me for what I did. From that day forward, I never stole a car again. Just 24 hours earlier, I had thought that I was going to steal cars forever because I enjoyed the rush so much, but when reality hit, I never looked down that road again.

My situation in life only became worse due to my run-in with the law. My father used drugs heavily again, and I was locked up in juvenile hall for missing my court appearance. Even though I was there for a week, it was the worst experience ever. First, I had no soap or comb, so for the first two days I didn't shower. In addition, I was in with kids who were staying there longer than I was and who felt like they had nothing to loose. Those are the most dangerous people in the world; the ones who don't care if they live or die. It was an interesting time in my life because I had to learn to walk a certain way, and I had to listen to whatever the correctional officers told me to do. They made us walk with our hands behind our backs, with our right hands over our left, in a straight line. If we disobeyed them in any way, we were sent to our room for the entire day. I don't want to spend the rest of my life here. It made me realize how much I enjoyed my freedom. Finally, the day came when I did not have to live under the confines of juvenile hall and I was released into my father's custody. I began to realize how my society worked; how it was designed to keep those who had to endure its impoverished ways trapped inside its clutches. My father took me home to the motel. He didn't seem to care that I had been in juvenile hall; I had to pay society what I owed it. My father continued using drugs, and I knew he was leaning towards getting rid of me once again.

I came home from school one day and, to my surprise, my father said, "I got laid off from my job. So you'll have to live with Jeanie again." I did not want to go back there. I felt bad that my father had lost his job and had to go live with one of his sisters, who did not want him around even when he had his job. I could tell that my father felt like he had lost control of his life. I did not want to go back to Jeanie's house; she was already bitter towards my family, especially me. The only reason she let me stay with her was to rub it in my face that I needed her. I would have been very content to live in a foster home if it had been an option, but I held in my pride and endured Jeanie's verbal abuse. I just had to find ways to escape the negative, bitter atmosphere in that house. Occasionally, I went to see my father when he lived with his sister, just to make sure that he was doing okay and not on drugs.

SURVIVAL

Education, education, education,
Go out and get it, cause there will soon be liberation.
But what about today?
My mama is on crack; no food in the house, and my hunger
grows day by day,
Yet education will eventually set me free.
Let's keep it real
At the age of nine, I have no father figure and my table is
missing a meal
Now what options do I face?
Go to school get an education and hope my hunger goes away.
Not a chance
There is no way in hell this book can fill my tummy
I'm not a dummy
Let's keep it real
I'm hungry now, so boxes of cereal I'll steal
Ah that's better
I can now go on
But don't think it's over, cause my hunger still grows strong
What is a child to do?
No mother, no father, so I'll turn to you
Yet you shut me down too
So I'm stranded in the dark
Shut out from Noah's ark
Left to drown in a sea of troubles
With no lifeguard to save my soul.
How bold
You expect me to go to school, when I can't even see the light
And do what's right
What about you leaders who won't even feed us
You expect me to look up to you
When you look down on me

Liberty.
I can't get pass my biological needs
Yet you expect me to pass a class and succeed
What is a child to do?
When you have tortured my kind
And blocked us out from the sunshine
Yes you, the powers that be
Yawl not all white, there is some who even look at me.
What a shame
Don't use my life as a game
It's precious
I'm just like you
I was just born into a manifested cycle, called the ghetto
Inequalities petrol, gasoline if you know what I mean.
Let's let the truth surface
You did this for a purpose
As my hunger grows and education I lack
Guided by ignorance and cursed cause I'm black
I am supposed to succeed.
You fail to mention I live in a world of greed
So I plead for help
Yet you look the other direction
Turned your back on me and denied me your protection.
Now the savage in me is free
Guiding me to a biological destiny
Food, clothes, and warm shelter
You begin to look at me as though I was helter skelter
A criminal.
I won't stop cause the hunger goes on
I speak for the youth
You can deny the lie but you can't deny the truth
This is a taste of my reality
Not sugar coated and definitely not a fallacy
This is what you created

A subculture, alienated, better yet segregated from the majority.

Now just cause you possess the authority, doesn't give you the right to control me

Lets go back to this thing called liberty

A hypocritical meaning that belittles me

It states that every man is free, an equal

Yet it excludes my people

Why lie when the truth is so clear

Is it fear?

Cause the reality is, I can co-exist with you

Have a better life and encourage my kids to see it through

But you think you figured out a way to keep me trapped

You infiltrated my lifestyle and had my phone tapped

So that you can study the way we work

And develop a plan to cause our life style to go berserk.

But see I was blessed

God possessed me with this thing called a third eye, so that I can see through this mess

This conflicted mentality that's been implanted in the minds of ghetto youth

Will be eradicated and so that they see the truth.

It's time to rearrange this blasphemous way of living

So that their minds get free

It's time to show them the truth, so that they see the opportunity

The opportunity to escape from this madness and end this sadness that's been going on for centuries

A life style that's sent thousands of our kind to penitentiaries.

But collectively, we can make a change

Now it might sound strange, but we can eradicate this lifestyle that was designed for us

And stop this madness that's been causing a fuss

So that as a people, we rise.

CHAPTER FIFTEEN

FROM HOUSE TO HOUSE AND SCHOOL TO SCHOOL

I remember going to my aunt's house to check on my father and actually having a good time. One day when I went to see him, he had received his welfare check and took me out to eat, and then gave me $40 to take back with me the next day. After our day together, we went back to my aunt's house to relax and talk, then nightfall hit. My father left the house and I knew where he was going. I hid my money deep in the sock that was still on my foot. I thought he would never find my money in that hiding spot, so I went to sleep. I woke up the next morning and the first thing I did was check to see if the money was there. To my surprise, he had found my hiding spot and had taken every cent. Everyone was still asleep, so I put on my shoes and caught the bus back to Jeanie's house without telling anyone I was leaving. I remember thinking I wouldn't ever trust anyone in my life! I figured if I couldn't trust my mom and father or anyone else I lived with, who could I trust? These people supposedly cared about me, and they were the first ones willing to steal from me. I didn't trust anyone, and that mistrust only intensified over the years. I began to keep to myself more and more as I grew older. I found ways to keep busy and to keep money in my pocket, and finally Jeanie agreed to let me and my brothers sell candy for a man in the neighborhood. This was a pinnacle point in my life because this man took kids from the local neighborhood and gave us jobs to help us make money. I really looked forward to this job, and I wanted to go out and sell more candy than anyone had ever sold. To our surprise, this man was anything but a nice guy. He cussed at us if we didn't sell as much as he thought we should have. He made sure that we knew he was the boss, and constantly threatened us by saying that if we tried to steal from him, we would pay a very heavy price.

We went door to door in rich neighborhoods because he knew that they were more likely to buy the candy if we had a catchy line. I would go up to a house and depending on if a man or woman answered, I had a line ready to feed them. This opportunity turned out to be a successful one for me. I worked off commission, so how much I made totally depended on me. But the job didn't last long because I got fed up with the way the man would talk to us. I figured if I wanted to be talked down to, I could just go home, so I quit. He knew he had made a mistake because I was his best seller. He tried to make me feel guilty enough to come back and work for him again, but I was smarter than that. He said, "If you quit this job, you'll quit every job you ever get! You can't handle pressure." When he figured out that all of his yelling and carrying on wouldn't convince me to come back, he said, "Get the hell out of my face before I slap the piss out of you." I went back to pumping gas and working at the hamburger stand, and I enjoyed every moment of it because I didn't have to put up with a person who tried to intimidate me.

I still lived with Jeanie and life was still the same whenever I was at home, but I dealt with it. My mother soon came to stay with us again; she could no longer afford to live in Los Angeles, and of course, the negativity level in the household skyrocketed once again. Jeanie and I still didn't get along and my high school years were going down the drain. I was kicked out of Jordan High School due to gang violence.

There was a hit out on my life because people associated me with Bernard, and he was in a rival gang to the one that predominately populated my school. My brother and I had gone to school together for one month before his life was threatened. After that, Bernard carried a gun to school everyday and was not afraid to go down in a blaze of gunfire if the rival gang decided to do something to us. I can recall one day at lunch when a gang member tried to get us to meet him behind the school so that we could fight. I was only in the ninth grade, so I was naive to the fact that it might have been a trap. He could have hidden a gun in the back of the school and was just waiting for us to slip up. I said, "Let's go," but Bernard was a little older and a lot more streetwise than I was. He said, "I know this guy's plan. We're gonna hang out in front of the school." He didn't tell me why at first, and I was anxious to fight. When the gang finally left, my brother told me why he didn't want to go back there, and then I understood.

The following week Bernard didn't come to school, and he never came back. I, on the other hand, stayed there, even though threats were being made on my life. Bernard pleaded with me not to go back, but I did. When the school caught wind of what was going on, they immediately rushed me out of the school, and expelled me because they thought that it was too dangerous for me to continue to go there. They sent me to a school even farther outside my district, and the bus stop was right across the street from Jordan High School. So instead of taking an hour to get to school everyday, it took two. While everyone else was asleep, I was catching a bus.

My new high school was a lot safer and they offered a better education. Although I struggled at Lakewood High, I still received a better education and learned a lot more. Lakewood was a predominantly white school, but there were splashes of multi-culturalism that decorated the student body. This was an ideal high school for me to attend, even though it could have used a little more diversity.

I quickly became acquainted with the few black people that attended my new school, and they welcomed me with open arms. It was interesting because the different ethnic groups hung out in specific areas of the school. There were unspoken boundaries between different groups. I accepted it and we did the same because it was the norm of the school. I became somewhat relaxed and settled into my new environment. Little did I know that my days in this privileged high school were coming to an abrupt end.

One of the other black kids in school was threatened by my size and would often make condescending remarks about my clothes, or any other flaw for that matter. He used to say, "Just 'cause you're big that doesn't mean I can't kick your ass." I never tried to punch him or make him feel inferior, but his insecurities overpowered his reason. I think he felt that just because he was in the eleventh grade and a little bit taller than I was, he could push me around. Despite all of his attempts to try and push my buttons, I avoided physical contact. I knew that if I got into a fight, I would be kicked out of this school, too and sent to the high school in my neighborhood, so I tried to avoid him completely. Then the day came when he laid his hands on me.

We were hanging out in our group, and he began torment-
ing me about the clothes I was wearing. That didn't really bother
me anymore; that was a battle I had fought my whole life. Then he
pushed the back of my head and told me I dressed like I was a bum.
That's where he made a mistake. I pretended it didn't bother me
when he pushed my head, but really it was just a delayed reaction.
I turned around and looked at him as he laughed, and out of
nowhere, I punched him directly in the face. He looked at me in
shock! I had shown no facial expressions when I hit him or as we
locked eyes. He became completely enraged, but this was exactly
what I wanted him to do because it gave me the upper hand; he was
trying to fight me out of anger rather than control.

He rushed me and I stepped to the side and punched him in
the exact same place. He rushed me again, and I punched him
again. He then began to settle down and re-think his strategy
because he desperately wanted to kick my a--, so we squared up
and went toe-to-toe. It was humorous, in a way. He grew even more
frustrated because I was smiling while we fought, but I couldn't
help it, he had been talking a ton of s--- saying, "I could kick your
a--." The reality was that I was kicking his. It took the entire secu-
rity force in the school to stop the fight. I was embarrassed after-
wards because I looked at our fight as entertainment for the benefit
of the rest of the student population, rather than having any real
meaning. We were sent to the office and once the principal found
out that I was involved, I was kicked out of his district. He expelled
me on the spot and sent me back to the ghetto where he thought I
belonged.

❧

When she found out that I was expelled, I knew that Jeanie would use this against me. She would always throw it in my face saying, "You're a screw-up. If you get kicked out of school, you'll never amount to anything." It just goes to show you that we all have a chance to make it. It's just whether or not you're willing to fight for something more than what you see every day.

I had to face Jeanie to tell her that I was expelled from my new high school. Granted, it had taken me a month, but I was finally kicked out. She was pissed off and told me that she didn't want me living with her anymore. I accepted what she said and got in contact with my father, who now lived with his girlfriend, Sharon, in South Central Los Angeles and went to live with him.

This was the turning point in my life. I didn't like the lady my father was dating; she was evil. She claimed to be a Christian, and she went to church every Sunday. When she came home, the devil was unleashed like a pack of hungry wolves after a deer. She complained about everything, and she was always angry about something. Sharon wanted things to go her way, but never really gained enough control of her life to see her ambitions through. She was angry at the world. There would be times when Sharon would not say a word to me because of what my father had done to her. She had two daughters who also lived in the same house, and they were just as crazy and immature as she was. Of course, I stayed away from home as much as possible.

Her daughter Aretha was fourteen years old and had a nine-month-old baby. She was pregnant with her second one and didn't really care. By the age of fifteen, Aretha had three kids and was well on her way to having more. She would run away from home and no one would see her for months. She knew that she could depend on her mother to help her support her kids. Sharon did whatever her daughters wanted her to do; my grandmother fell into the same trap. Unfortunately, Aretha's younger sister looked up to her and was slowly but surely following her example.

Her sister, Sharmony, controlled the household. She threw temper tantrums that drove her mother and the rest of us insane. Sharmony was only thirteen years old, but she did whatever she wanted and her mother couldn't do anything about it. Sharmony was the type of girl who liked to get under people's skin just to piss them off. She was just as evil as her mother and. sometimes worse. She would even steal clothes from me and give them to her boyfriend. I couldn't trust her at all, so I put a padlock on my bedroom door. Sharmony wanted to be just like her sister and would do stupid things to get attention. I can remember catching Sharmony and her boyfriend having sex right outside my bedroom door, but I walked by as though I didn't see a thing. I kept my distance from her and she kept her distance from me. The only thing we shared was a mutual animosity. It seemed that no matter where I lived, people were always upset about something.

This household was just as bad as the one in which I had previously lived; there were just fewer people. I could not relate to anyone in the house, and I never tried to. I would come home after school and go straight to my room without saying a word to anyone. I came out when it was time to eat, and then went right back into my room. This is when I began to take advantage of school because I saw it as an escape route.

Peace of mind is a very valuable thing. I started checking out books on black history from the school library. I remember reading my first book, The Autobiography of Harriet Tubman. That was such a powerful experience for me because I felt as if I, myself, was on the journey of the Underground Railroad. This book inspired me to read many more, each allowing me to leap into other people's lives. I stayed with my father and Sharon until I graduated from junior high school, and then I went on to the local high school, where I began to play football and found another way to escape from my reality.

When I entered Thomas Jefferson High School, I knew I would graduate there. The school welcomed me in with open arms, and it seemed like I would benefit from the curriculum. My middle school physical education teacher had suggested that I tryout for the football team that he coached at Jefferson, so I did. I was welcomed by the football team and was quickly adopted into its family. This was nothing more than another outlet for me and a way for me to release the aggression that had been building inside of me for the last few years. I now had an opportunity to have fun and stay away from home at the same time.

Incidentally, Jefferson High was a joke. I had teachers who didn't know the lifestyle of their students, so they never taught worthwhile material. I had one teacher, Ms. Fadler, who was the weirdest teacher I had ever had. She always came to class in a frantic or chaotic way and tried to teach the lesson. She mumbled her words, possibly because she had a speech impediment, and on top of that, she ate while she talked. My first impression of her was that she was a crack head. I thought she used drugs and that she taught us while she was high. Finally, she would come to class, explain what she wanted us to do, and then return to her office. She did not monitor our class or correct our work; she had a student in the class do that for extra credit.

One incident occurred where my best friend and I were being obnoxious in class. The class was already out of control, but on this particular day, we were extremely disruptive. Ms. Fadler tried explaining the assignment and she became very frustrated. She saw that my friend and I were acting the most obnoxiously of the group, so she decided to make an example out of us. She kicked us out of the class for the entire semester. We didn't believe that she could do such a thing; we were only four weeks into the semester and were already kicked out of a class we needed to graduate. We never tried to re-enter it; we just waited to see what our report cards would look like. When we received our grades, we both were given B's in a class we never attended. We laughed and didn't say a word about it to anyone for fear that our real grades would be exposed. I knew that this high school wouldn't challenge me, but I didn't do anything to try to find another. I was comfortable in my setting and was not about to relocate again.

I took advantage of the opportunity I had because I knew once school was over for the day, I would have to go home and put up with Sharon and her family. My father and Sharon argued on a regular basis and this only brought more tension to our living situation. I finally had an outlet; I never had to be home. The only time I came home was at night after football practice. My new extracurricular activity worked out great; I could relieve my stress and stay away from those who caused it. Yet obstacles always seemed to descend out of the clear blue sky.

My father and Sharon broke up because my father was stealing money from her and buying drugs with it. He would spend all of his money then try to spend all of hers, so she kicked us out, but my father had another girlfriend on the side and they decided to rent a house in a nice neighborhood in Compton. I secretly hoped that my father would marry this woman. Her name was Renee, and she was the nicest girlfriend my father ever had and the nicest woman I ever met. Besides her gentle nature, she had a good job and helped our family at all costs.

Renee and my father had known each other all of their lives and had even dated at one time. Compared to life at home, it was paradise; it was the highlight of our young lives. We would go over to their house twice a year and she treated us like kings. We had everything we wanted: food, clothes, and a warm house. We would sit back on their couch and watch movies all day; something we never did when at home. In addition, at my mother's house my siblings and I always needed clothing. My brothers and I shared clothes because we did not have enough to last us the whole year. We switched off every other day to make it appear as if we possessed a plethora of garments, but it wasn't like that at my father's. Renee had a good job and took care of my father, so when we went over to their house, she spoiled us rotten. She gave us money, took us to get ice cream, and more. Renee did the little things for us that other kids took for granted. We wished she was our mother and dreaded the idea of going back home.

Renee was considerate of all of us and always gave me the positive reinforcement I had been looking for all my life. I remember wanting a snake, and she and my father decided to let me buy one. Even though she was scared of it, she was still willing to let me keep it in her house. She did whatever she could to make sure that we had a happy household. My father even stopped using drugs so that she would be happy. I always wanted this life; it was a dream come true. We always had food in the refrigerator, and I didn't really have to worry about anything. I was given an allowance, and taken care of like it was a real family, but these days soon ended and we were thrown back into our hell.

After about six months, my father started using drugs again and Renee was not about to put up with that in her house, so she packed up and left us. She took all of her furniture and that pretty much left our house bare. This, of course, only intensified my father's drug use and made my life worse. I thought for sure that my father was going to stay off drugs this time; she had given us everything we needed to survive, including a happy family. But he could not stand the fact that Renee earned more money then he did, so this was his way of rebelling against her.

He stayed out until all hours of the night, and Renee and I would stay up waiting for him to come home. I remember her saying, "I can't take much more of your father and his behavior. I just can't trust him anymore."

"If you decide to go, I'll miss you," I said.

"You have to hang in there, Eboni."

I did not want to see Renee leave because she was responsible for our happiness, but deep down in my heart I understood why she wanted to leave, and if I had a chance to escape the drugs that plagued my life, I would have left, too. Eventually she left because my father stole money from her. She gave me her new number at her new house, "You can keep in touch if you need anything." She even paid us visits on occasion, but did not stay for long because she could not stand to see my father in that condition. Eventually, I lost her number and never saw her again.

After awhile, Bernard came to stay with my father and me. He attended a correctional school in the neighborhood, but it was nice to be around him again. Bernard was a good addition to our house because we could use each other to vent. My father's drug habit was getting more and more intense and we were on the verge of being evicted from our home.

Bernard and I had just received a laptop computer as a present from a lady at my high school. I was so excited because I had never had anything that expensive before. I hid it under my bed so that my father wouldn't find it and try to sell it, but again my plan was foiled when he found it and sold it for drugs. I never confronted him but Bernard did.

Then one beautiful, sunny day my mother showed up with Travie and wanted to take Bernard to Las Vegas with her. She needed someone to protect her because she was mixed up in a food stamp selling scheme. She would go to Vegas and sell food stamps for real money. My father did not want Bernard to go because he had been missing school and didn't deserve to go. Of course, this pissed Bernard off and he told our father, "Benny, you don't deserve to be our father. You always steal things from us to buy drugs."

My mother, the drama queen, then jumped in. "Yeah, Benny you can go to hell because they're my kids." (Like she was any better).

Bernard then asked my father, "Why did you sell the laptop?"

"I didn't sell it," he said, but you could see the guilt in his face. My mother asked the same question, and this only pissed him off more; he pushed my mother on the ground in our driveway, and Bernard, reacting out of frustration, pushed my father. Then the fight broke out.

Benny rushed Bernard and my brother punched my father in the face. Fists flew back and forth and Benny wound up with the short end of the stick. This infuriated him so much that he went into the house and grabbed a baseball bat. Travie was screaming frantically at me to stop the fight, but, I did nothing. I stayed perched on the car as if nothing was going on. I felt bitter towards my father for all of the things he had done to me, and I felt like he and my brother needed to fight. I was totally content with letting the fight continue. Travie was pissed at me because I had a nonchalant attitude about the whole incident, and the neighbor looked on as the fight escalated. My father chased my brother down the street with the bat, but I stayed on the car because I knew that he couldn't catch him, and at this point in my life I didn't or couldn't care anymore.

I was fed up with my parents using drugs and putting their children through such a heart-wrenching life. I guess I felt that they deserved anything that happened to them, and I wouldn't have any sympathy for them. They put us through hell, and we didn't deserve that. We were just kids who didn't know what life had to offer, and they didn't spend the time to teach us how to maneuver life's obstacles. Instead, they let us carry the weight of their existence, without even letting us lean on them for support.

After the fight, my father kicked my brother out, and he had to go live with my mother at Jeanie's house. Travie and I stayed with my father and continued to endure the drugs and the stealing of our personal things. My father started dating Sharon again, so my little brother and I knew that it was only a matter of time before we were going to move to Los Angeles. Benny had not been keeping up with the rent, and we knew that an eviction notice was going to arrive any day.

The day had come. We came home from school and Benny said, "We're moving to L.A. to live with Sharon." I had already known what to expect because I had lived there once before. My little brother, on the other hand, had no idea what he was getting into, so I briefed him on what he was about to go through. Knowing that he had no choice, he packed his bags and joined me in the new hell hole. I dreaded going to live with Sharon because I knew I would have to get rid of my snake. I did not want to part with my favorite animal; it was the only loyal thing I'd ever had in my life. As soon as we brought it into the house, Sharon said that we had to get rid of it because she wouldn't have the devil's creature living in her home, as if she wasn't his finest creation. I had to figure out a place that would take in my snake. Fortunately, my science teacher let me keep it in his class; this way I could take care of it every day. I despised Sharon for making me get rid of my snake, and I refused to speak to her.

Life went as expected in the house of hell until one day my father threw my brother and me a curve ball. Benny and Sharon went away for a weekend and came back married. I couldn't believe it; my father was actually married to this lady. We just pretended that we were happy for them and life went on as it had.

Nothing had changed. Sharon was still as b----y as ever, and her daughters were as crazy as ever. Aretha now had three kids and was only seventeen years old, and Sharmony was beginning to run in the streets a little more than before. She came and went as she pleased, and her mother didn't do anything to stop it. I continued playing football and doing whatever I had to do to stay away from home. My coach knew my predicament and helped me out as much as he could.

DESTINY

What controls your destiny?
What determines your fate?
Though you live in a society of hate,
It ain't too late to break free.
The evil that exist in this universe is a curse,
But what's worse, if you let it get you down your last ride
might be in a hearse.
The vision is there,
You just have to let it guide you to your dreams.
Help you be what you want to be, so that you may ride your
streams.
God didn't place you here to be the victim of the gun, always
on the run;
He placed you here to have fun, and share the wisdom you've
learned with your son.
So that the cycle ends.
Now it depends on you
Do you want to end this tragedy that young black men be
going through?
I do.
That's why I'm trying to make our gray skies blue,
I want this cycle to die.
So that my people have every opportunity to fly.
Fly to the endless land untouched by the evils of man.
Now I hope you understand
That I mean what I say,
This cycle ends today.
Walk with me and I'll show you the way,
The way to the life you can't see,
So that you can grasp your destiny.
Now the torch has been lit
And to make shore you never forget.

This is branded in your heart
Like a work of art
Now it's your turn to share the light,
So that your seeds can do what's right.
I've done my deed,
Now it's up to you to succeed.

CHAPTER SIXTEEN

SOMEONE TO BELIEVE IN ME

Coach Johnson would let me and another player—my best friend, Isaac—cut his grass to make a little bit of extra money. I looked at Coach Johnson as a father figure who tried to make my life a little bit easier. He invited us to his house, so that we could cut his grass and to check up on us. If he didn't need his grass cut, he would give us money anyway to make sure our bare necessities were being met. I think he did this to keep us away from selling drugs or doing something stupid that would ruin our lives forever. Coach Johnson was a mentor to Isaac and me because he told us about the realities of life, and what we needed to do to succeed in an environment such as ours. He did everything in his power to assure us that we were on the right track to graduation. I believe he looked at us as though we were his own kids; he was the first to discipline us if we messed up in a class or did anything that was demeaning to ourselves. He made sure we kept our goals in mind and continued moving forward to accomplish them.

Coach Johnson was also the dean of students, responsible for the discipline of our school. His direct approach was that he told you how he felt regardless of how it might make you feel. He refused to sugar coat the realities of life because he knew that it wouldn't be sugar coated when it caught you off guard. I looked up to him for his honesty. If I wanted to know the truth about something, whether it was about football or school, he would be brutally honest. That's what made Coach Johnson so special; he prepared us for the real world, let us know what to expect, and taught us how to react. He showed you through his actions how much he loved you and cared about your future. Looking back on my experiences with Coach Johnson, they were all positive ones because even if he told me something I didn't want to hear, it was the truth.

Coach Johnson was the type of man who never turned his back on you, even when you turned your back on yourself. He was always there as a mentor, as a father figure and as a friend. He was the one responsible for bringing my best friend, Isaac, and me together. I remember him telling us on the day we met, "You guys will wind up best friends for life, and no one will ever be able to break the bond of your friendship." He made sure that when I was invited to go to his house to cut the grass, Isaac was right along with me. We became close through Coach Johnson and our friendship continues to grow stronger and stronger to this day.

Cozch Chapel was another coach who had a strong impact in my life as well. Coach Chapel was the richest coach I had ever met. He would come to school in three-piece suits and with jewelry wrapped allover his fingers. He was in his mid-fifties, but had the spirit of a twenty-five-year-old. He would lift weights with me and would play basketball and football with us. He was another man in my life who reinforced the notion that I could be anything I wanted to be, as long as I worked hard for it. He drove a Rolls Royce to school and had a house in the hills of Palace Verdi, overlooking the ocean. He would invite us over to cut his grass as well, and pick up around his yard and paid us for it. He always took us to breakfast before we got down to work. He showed me that I could have the finer things in life.

I asked him, "How did you become so rich?"

"I bought houses, fixed them up, and sold them at a profit. There is always money out there, but you have to be willing to go out and work for it," he said.

He made sure that I was on top of my schoolwork, because he saw promise in me. He believed in me and knew that I could make it if I just kept my head on straight. He and Coach Johnson motivated me to do my best in whatever I chose to do, and taught me that that was the only way I would get ahead. I didn't know at the time that these things would stick in my head until I began to grow older and could look back at the conversations we had and then was able to realize that I was using what he said in my day-to-day experiences. We shared common interests—snakes and weightlifting. After I no longer could keep my snake at school because of safety issues, Coach Chapel agreed to buy it from me for a reasonable price because he liked me so much.

I remember him sitting in the back of the end zone during one of our football games when I picked up a fumble and ran it back for a touchdown. He jumped out of his seat to congratulate me. He never showed emotion, and it excited me. I appreciated them for taking time out of their lives to show me that they cared that much about my success when no one else did. They helped instill a hope and a belief in me, a belief that I could do anything I put my mind to; and that helped mold me into the man I am today. Coach Johnson was the one who encouraged me to get into classes that would prepare me for college and challenge the way I thought.

At his prompting, I checked into classes in the "humanities curriculum." These classes combined science, English, history and politics to form a unified curriculum that incorporated all of these subjects to allow for a cohesive way of thinking. The primary benefit from my humanities experience was that I met Debra Constance, a woman who worked at the Jon Douglas Real Estate Company.

Jon Douglas had paid a visit to our high school during my sophomore year, and I was assigned to give him a tour around campus. It seemed like I was his bodyguard, and the school administration wanted me to make sure that no one bothered him. He was the owner of a multimillion-dollar real estate company with offices throughout southern California. He was visiting our school as a guest speaker, his topic being setting and achieving your goals. As I showed him around the school and became acquainted with him, I found him to be a truly genuine person and someone who really appreciated what he had accomplished. Here he was, a middle-aged white man in an inner-city high school, telling kids to push forward towards their goals. It was strange to me that he had an interest in our school, rather than have one in a predominantly white school in a nice neighborhood. To be honest, I was dumfounded by the whole situation, but once I got to know him and understood that he didn't start out his life with everything handed to him—that he truly had to work hard for the things he had—I began to understand that he knew what it felt like to struggle.

The week following his visit, I received a card from him thanking me for taking the time out of my schedule to give him a tour of the campus and making sure that he was safe. I thought at that moment, if he had taken the time out of his day to appreciate what I had done for him, which was nothing, maybe he was truly a generous man.

At this time in my life, I was looking for a job and hadn't had any luck finding one, until Debra, his right hand woman, encouraged me to ask him for a job, so I did. I called Jon Douglas and asked him if he had any job openings anywhere in his business and he answered, "Of course; no problem." He gave me a number to call, and I instantly had a position. This was the beginning of a new perspective on life.

At the same time I received the real estate job, I also got a job working at Taco Bell. I decided to work at the real estate company during the day, and the graveyard shift at Taco Bell. The real estate job offered all types of different avenues of learning; it brought me into contact with a world outside of my community. Even though it took me four hours to get to and from work everyday, I was enthusiastic about what I was doing. I had to take four busses to reach my destination, but it was all worth it because I learned so much by escaping the confines of my community. At Jon Douglas Real Estate Company, I worked in the corporate office and assisted in any department that needed help getting its daily routine done. I helped the clerical department in ordering supplies; I assisted the accounting department in assuring that all of the financial needs were met and accurate; I helped in the ad department and learned how they published ads in the local newspapers. It was an incredible experience. During this time, I figured out that I could do anything my boss could do—all I had to do was watch and learn.

Linda, my boss, had a college degree and earned $45,000 a year. I figured all I needed to do to get to that level was go to college and get a degree. It was exciting to me to know that I could do the things that people twice my age were doing. I also compared and contrasted the two jobs at which I worked. I realized that I was getting paid less money to work harder at Taco Bell than I did working at Jon Douglas. I realized that Jon Douglas paid well, but wasn't nearly as hard or labor intensive. So I stepped back, looked at the two positions and asked myself which one I would rather be in: the one that offered no opportunity in a dangerous setting or the one that offered a world of opportunity in a comfortable environment?

I knew what it felt like to be hungry and homeless, but I could only imagine, what would it be like to have the things I wanted and needed in life? Do I want to stay in the 'hood amongst drugs and poverty? Do I want to go to college and make something of myself? This is when I made the ultimate decision in my life—college. I had finally seen the light that everyone talked about, and it would guide me to an infinite amount of opportunity, and I couldn't wait to embark on the journey. Though my reality in the 'hood still haunted me, I knew that one day I would make the most of my opportunities. My goals suddenly seemed closer, and I knew that I could achieve them.

Soon after I had this revelation, I quit my job at Taco Bell and put all my effort into becoming the best I could be at Jon Douglas. I now had a destination, and I felt like I had some control over my fate. I had an opportunity to compare the two different lifestyles that existed for me and was given a choice. I was given the choice to continue living in the ghetto or the choice to work towards getting out and being something better. I was introduced to a positive atmosphere, and I loved it! Jon Douglas Company opened my eyes to a new world and I was mesmerized by what it had to offer. I was tired of drugs, poverty and death, and I now had an opportunity to one day escape its clutches. For the time being, at least, I could escape for up to eight hours a day on my school vacations. I felt myself getting caught up in a destructive thought process, and this was my opportunity to break free from that norm. I began to look at football as a vehicle for getting out of the 'hood and into college. I started to figure out that I could use football as a tool for changing my life. It would become my escape route from the 'hood and nothing was more valuable than that.

Football became my focus when I wasn't working at Jon Douglas. I knew that if I excelled in football, I would get an opportunity to go to college for free and make something of myself. Football became my driving force for success, and it brought with it a world of opportunity. When the letters started pouring in from different colleges across the United States, I knew that my window of opportunity was opening a little wider, and I knew that all I had to do was keep working hard and it would lead to promising results. I was blessed with a strong body that allowed me to dominate my opponents. All of my hard work in the weight room was finally paying off on the field. Even the aggression I felt toward my parents and family became fuel for accomplishing my goals. Football became my ticket out, and Coach Johnson did his best to put my name in the ears of the college coaches who came to recruit me. He worked overtime to make sure that I got the best opportunity I could. That is why I appreciate him so much. He was there for me and helped me achieve my goals. My high school career flourished, and I continued to work hard, even though my mother and father continued to use drugs.

My father continued on his petty mission of getting high as often as he could. He really didn't follow my football career at all.

Throughout my entire time in high school, he only showed up to one of my games, and I am not sure if he even stayed for the whole time. He didn't show much interest in my extracurricular activities, and at the time, that really bothered me. After the first year of him not showing up to any of my football games or track meets, I became immune to the feeling of being let down, and no longer expected to see his face in the crowd anymore. It even stopped bothering me when he forgot to ask me how my game went. I had my life to live and he had his. I never asked him what he did with his day and he never bothered to ask me what I did with mine, but at least we still got along.

I didn't let football interfere with how well we got along with each other; it just meant that we didn't have that king of father-son relationship. We had more of a passing relationship, meaning if we ran into each other, we would talk but if we didn't, it wouldn't bother us one bit. We stayed in our own worlds, living separate lives, but in some ways that was good for me. I didn't agree with the way he lived his life, and he wasn't concerned with what I did with mine, as long as I didn't get into trouble. There were times when he would stop using drugs, and I enjoyed interacting with him during those windows a little more than usual. I wanted him to know that I liked the way he was when he wasn't using. I enjoyed seeing him healthy and free from the toxic waste that was slowly killing him. I enjoyed being able to talk to him without worrying that he was, later on, going to get high. He was a free spirit when he was off drugs and that made him more approachable, but the joy wouldn't last long; he was soon right back where he started.

When he used drugs, he became zoned-out from society and in a trance-like state; all he thought about was his next high. He was looking for that ultimate high and was not going to stop until he reached his destination. It killed me to see him killing himself; to watch your parent moving closer and closer to his death—a fate I wouldn't wish on my worst enemy. He had to realize on his own that he was the only one who could change his condition. My mother was in the same predicament, and she faced the same end if she didn't stop using drugs as well. My mother was trapped in the cycle of the ghetto, lost in her addiction. Like my father, she only came to one of my games.

We were forced to deal with ridicule from our peers who watched our lives going down the drain. We as children had to bear the whips and scorn of the drug world, and one of its most devastating side effects, poverty. Drugs had plagued my family my entire life and while in high school, they continued to haunt me. I just bore it for as long as I had to, and waited to be free. I didn't care who didn't come to my games anymore, and I couldn't have cared less about what my parents were doing. It was obvious that they didn't care about what I did with my life, just so long as I stayed out of theirs'. I became immune to this type of self-destructive behavior, and learned how to endure its black rain.

THE GAME

You come to college full of aspiration
Ready to play your first game, overwhelmed with determina-
tion
You play your heart out and give your all
To not play in that next game, you can't stand at all.
You ask your coach what can you do to get on the field
He gives you a response, but refuses to keep it real
So your frustration grows
You begin to slip in school & nobody knows.
You thought that you could come and start
But you were snatched from the field cause you could not play
the part
So now your pissed and looking for ways to escape
Giving up on life and letting another man determine your
fate.
You begin to let your grades fall
All because you let a coach convince you that you couldn't ball
You wanted to play but unfortunately you got played
That's the way the cracker crumble, but don't let it stop you
from getting paid.
You let him shut your mind off from that knowledge
Causing your grades to drop, now he has a reason to kick you
out of college
He is itching to give your scholarship away
So he lied to you, told you that you'll never make it, and
another game you'll never play.
So you believed it
Gave up on life and now you ready to quit
You let the game play you, instead of you playing the game
What a shame.
You should have looked in that mirror you shattered
Rearranged your aspirations and sorted out the things that

mattered.
Ask yourself what you can do to make yourself better
Or what type of road you have to pave to get your cheddar
What can you do to play?
Sit on the couch, drown in your sorrows, or get up and take
advantage of the day
You are the one who controls your fate
Don't give anyone the chance to dictate.
Your reflection is the captain of your soul
It determines if you succeed or lay homeless in the cold.
Be accountable for your actions
And then you'll grow with satisfaction
Take advantage of college, and gain that knowledge.
It is the gift that makes you whole
It unlocks the minds secrets, so the mysteries can unfold
Don't let the game play you, see it through
Because the outcome of your life is only determined by you
That's the game.

CHAPTER SEVENTEEN

A WAY OUT

Football was the vehicle that allowed me to escape the ghetto. I knew that football could put distance between me and my parents' drug habits, and I would no longer have to worry about watching my back when I walked down the street if I got a scholarship. Football was it; I just had to grab the opportunity and run with it. My sophomore season went great, but it was time to take the pre-SAT, and I was not a good at taking tests.

When I received my test scores, they were just as I expected; I had not done well at all. Actually, I did horribly. I had the lowest score in my class, which, of course, made me feel like an idiot. I thought that that was the end of my chances to go to a university right out of high school, and I didn't know what I was going to do until my coach told me about Proposition 48. Prop 48 means if you meet the GPA standards to get into college, but not the SAT scores, you can still be admitted, but you have to pay for your first year of school and you then have the opportunity to earn an athletic scholarship the following year. I had no idea how I was going to be able to pay my tuition when I was just about the poorest kid in my high school, but then Coach mentioned financial aid. The poorer you are, the more money you get from the government! I just had to worry about getting accepted to a college first. This gave me hope, and I continued to work hard in school to make sure I had the highest GPA I could! I also worked hard to improve my SAT scores just in case, by a small miracle, I could pass them.

I've since learned that the SAT is just another obstacle designed to keep kids trapped in the 'hood. It doesn't measure the drive you have to succeed in life; it just measures what someone thinks your ability is to make it in college, and your economic background. It's biased. I couldn't even understand the wording of the test; it was not written in the way I was taught to speak in my neighborhood or in my school. I thought it was a joke and that some of the words they used were not real. The test made me feel inferior, as if I didn't learn a thing in high school. I took it again in my junior year of high school, and never took it again after that. My score on the SAT was a 470, which is probably the lowest score you can have. I needed a 700 to pass, and I was nowhere near that score. I was told that the ACT was a better test to take, and that I should focus on taking that. I focused my attention on the ACT and hoped that I would pass it so that I wouldn't have to worry about paying for my first year of school.

After the colleges got a hold of my SAT results, a lot of them dropped me, leaving me with very limited choices. Being recruited by all the major universities had been heaven to me because it offered a world of opportunity to choose from, but with my selections narrowed down by the test, I had fewer options. Fortunately, there were a few schools that still had faith in me and that kept my fire burning. Time was running out.

I visited the University of Southern California first because it was the school I wanted to attend the most. It had been my favorite university since I was a little boy. My host took me to places I had never been, and I had lived in L.A. for seventeen years.

They treated me like a king, and I enjoyed every second of it. I was able to get to know Keshawn Johnson really well and all of the rest of the USC football players. I knew I wanted to attend this school, but since I didn't pass my SAT, so it soon faded as an option, too. They wanted me to go to junior college for a year, but I didn't want to do that because I had to get out of the 'hood.

Then I went to Kansas University where a former high school teammate was attending. I didn't like him so I didn't give the school much consideration. I enjoyed the people and the environment, but I didn't think I could put up with my old teammate for five years. Then I took a trip to Washington State University. I really enjoyed my trip to WSU because at the time when I was recruited, they had the number one defense in the nation and were on their way to a bowl game. I can honestly say that, at first, I didn't want to attend WSU because it seemed to me that they suffered from a lack of ethnic diversity among staff and students. I felt like I wouldn't fit in if I signed the letter of intent, so I continued on my campus visits.

After WSU, I traveled on to San Jose State University to learn about their program. The moment I arrived on campus, I knew that I would never go to school there. It reminded me too much of home; there were actually Crips and Bloods in northern California. I couldn't believe it. We went to a nightclub and the first thing that happened was a fight, then shortly after that, they started shooting, and I had flashbacks of home. The whole time I was there, I just agreed to whatever the coaches were saying as long as they didn't ask me to commit to their program.

My final trip was to Hawaii. It took a lot for me to get this trip because the coaches worried that I just wanted a free vacation to there, which was, in part true, but I didn't want them to know that! I pretended to show interest so I could see what Hawaii was like. I mostly just wanted to know what it was like to be in Hawaii; I wanted to see if it was like what I had seen on television. When I arrived on the campus, its beauty captivated me. I knew that it wasn't the place for me. It seemed as if I was isolated on a desert island and had no way of getting off—I felt completely secluded from the real world.

They kept encouraging me to keep taking the SAT again and told me that maybe I would pass them, but I didn't have that much confidence in myself. I didn't want to make my decision when it came down to it because I was afraid of making the wrong one. Then it finally clicked; I needed to get out of my environment and the only way I was going to do that was to go to WSU. The other universities offered me opportunities, but WSU was a PAC 10 school, far from L.A., and my family would be able to see me on television. USC was just a fantasy that I needed to let go of; it wasn't the best school for me, because it would have kept me confined to the environment I was trying to escape.

If I had stayed in southern California, I still had my parents and their problems. I knew that my mother would have been at the university all the time, bothering me about what was going on in her life. I figured if I signed at WSU, I could truly start my own life and finally made my decision. I knew that it was the best answer to my problems.

I believed that signing with WSU would help me become the person I wanted to be. All I had to do was make sure that I utilized the university's resources to the best of my ability. I finished my senior year, growing more and more excited in anticipation of my new environment. Sometimes I called my recruiting coach three times a week to see if I could come to campus earlier than other recruits could. I wanted to get out as soon as possible and even if it were just one day earlier, that would have been a blessing. I just wanted to get out of the 'hood as fast as I could. I wanted to start my own life as soon as God gave me the opportunity. Now I began to see the light at the end of the tunnel, and I was running as fast as I could towards it.

Finally, the recruiting coach gave me the answer that I was waiting for; he told me I could fly up on August 17, 1995. I can't begin to describe the happiness I felt when he gave me that news. I was nervous because I thought that something horrible would happen to me before I had an opportunity to escape into my new life. I thought that I would be caught in the crossfire of the ghetto or that the coach would tell me that the school didn't approve my admittance. I was nervous from the moment he told me I could come until the moment I got on the plane. Even then, I started worrying that the plane would crash.

As my family and I parted, there were no tears or sad goodbyes. There was just, "Hope you have a nice time. Keep in touch." That was enough for me because I wanted to get the hell out of that place as soon as possible. I got on the airplane and slept the whole trip because I wanted the time to pass so quickly. I arrived in Pullman, Washington on the morning of the seventeenth and was overwhelmed with excitement. The other recruits and one of the coaches came to pick me up. I already felt the freedom from the ghetto. I had control over my life, and I was willing to take full responsibility for my future. I was tired of playing the puppet for my family, when I could make a life for myself. I didn't realize what I had missed out on until I arrived.

When in college, one of the most pressing issues for a student is how he is going to get home for the holidays to see his family, and this never even occurred to me. In fact, I didn't want to go home, and I didn't realize how much I was missing out until I spent the holidays with friends and their families and began to see why they were so special to them. The joy of the holidays really revolves around a feeling of security. This is a feeling that people generally get from being "around their loved ones." I feel the most secure when I am away from my family. To me, my family represents negativity, drama, and self-pity. The very things that I despise and the very things you try to escape for the holidays. Needless to say, I haven't booked my flight home for this Christmas or plan to for any other holiday in the near future.

The "Prop 48s" had to come early because we needed to take a test so that we could be placed in the correct classes. I was intimidated because I tended to suffer from test anxiety, and I was scared that my test score would be so low that they would tell me that I had to go home. I took the test and was able to stay at WSU, so I pressed forward with my education. It was now time to register for classes and all I could think about was business administration. I was horrible at math, but I didn't care; I wanted to go into business, so that I wouldn't wind up in the ghetto again. I knew that a business degree would lead to a great job.

The first week I was there, I explored my surroundings. I walked allover campus and learned where all my classes were going to be so that I wouldn't be late. I even walked over to football practice and met all the players. I couldn't practice my first year because I was a "Prop 48," but I still wanted to establish a relationship with my teammates. I had to earn my scholarship academically, but I was willing to do what it took.

I knew that there would be some challenges in earning my scholarship, but I was willing to face those challenges in order to succeed in life. I knew I would have to get a job to support myself, and I was willing to do that; whatever it took to keep me out of the ghetto and away from the drugs that had followed me all my life. I knew that there were a lot of people who thought that I wouldn't make it in an institution like WSU, but I was aiming to prove to myself that I could. I knew that others were skeptical about my abilities because of my background, but I didn't let that stop me from doing what I was put there to do, which was succeed in every way.

Once school started, I expected it to be so hard that I wouldn't be able to keep up with all my classmates, yet to my surprise I was wrong. College was easier than high school. They gave students the tools needed to complete the assignments; they even offered tutors, people who were dedicated to seeing that you understood the material. This was more than I had ever expected. They gave you the tools for success. I thought I was in heaven. Although I struggled in one of my classes, my teacher was more than willing to make sure that I understood the material. She also spent time helping me study for the exams. She gave me reason to believe that there were people in Pullman who actually cared about the success of their students. She made me believe in myself even more than before. With her help, I went from an F to a C+, which opened for me a brand new method of studying and understanding the material.

My first semester was going great, but there were some teachers and family members who still doubted my ability to succeed in the classroom. I didn't let that stop me though; I kept fighting hard for the goals I had set out to accomplish, and I felt more and more in control, until the black rain that had been coming down all my life, hit again. When it rains, it pours. One day after a test on which I did really well, my coach called me into his office. I was happy and feeling good because I had just earned an A. When I walked into his office, he told me that my brother had just been shot and killed.

BERNARD

I can't begin to explain how much I miss you;
You are a part of me and understand what we've been
through.
You're my blood
And to see you gone causes rainstorms and floods.
The emptiness I felt when I was told you'll never grow old
Destroyed a part of me, as I lay out in the cold.
You fell victim to the hood, how could it be
I will never again hear your voice, your face I will never
again see?
I thought we'd share old memories together,
Failed by the ills of the 'hood, which destroyed our forever.
I still can't believe that God took you away
I knew we had to die one day, but Lord why today?
I guess it was bound to happen
Living in the 'hood, every night somebody start capping.
See your luck ran out bra' and those six bullets turned you
blue.
Not you,
As these tear drops flood my face.
I ponder and wonder who placed us in this cruel place.
They took your life from me,
Added you as another statistic, and threw your memories to
sea.
Never looking back,
To them your worth is nothing and it's because you're black.
Yet to me you're everything,
You mean the world to me and to think of you is exciting.
Only time will tell when I see you at the cross roads,
The day of grace that will lift this heavy load
I moan for you.

Chapter Eighteen

Bernard

I had just heard the words that I had feared my entire life. My brother had been shot, and those words still echo in my mind. When my coach told me, I burst into tears and fell against the wall in his office. I couldn't stop crying. I couldn't believe what he had just told me. I immediately knew it was Bernard because Peanut was in jail at the time. My coach tried to comfort me, but I just curled up in a corner in his office and cried. He kept asking me if I needed him to get me home so that I could go to the funeral, but I couldn't give him a response. After I stopped crying, I said, "I'm going to my room."

He asked me, if I wanted him to call my father and I said, yes. When my father answered the phone, I broke down in tears again, "Dad, is it true."

When he answered, yes, I dropped the phone. I still couldn't believe what was happening. My brother was dead and no one knew who did it.

Benny told me that Bernard had gone to get something to eat around three o'clock in the morning. He was trying to start his car, and finally got it started, when two guys approached on the passenger side, where his girlfriend was sitting, and started shooting out of control. His girlfriend was shot in the face, and Bernard was shot twice in the head and four other times in the body. The coroner said he had died instantly. I started bawling once again because the thought of my brother lying dead across the steering wheel of his car, the horn blowing, it blew my mind. I wanted vengeance. I told my father that I wasn't coming to the funeral because I was afraid I would do something stupid. I knew that if I saw my brother lying dead in that casket, I would have gone insane. I refused to go to the funeral. I knew that his friends and I would have plotted to kill the ones who murdered my brother. I felt the rage building up inside of me, so the best thing for me was to stay in Pullman and mourn on my own, rather than winding up in jail or lying right alongside him. Before I hung up, I told my father, "I'll talk to you later." I needed a chance to think about what had just happened.

I left my coach's office with my head hung low, so that I wouldn't have to see anyone on the way to my dorm. When I arrived at my room, I closed the door and started crying all over again. The reality of losing Bernard was too much, and the way he was taken still haunts me. It seemed like an eternity before I reached my dorm because a million things raced through my mind. I was thinking, this is impossible. I could kill the murderers that had the nerve to kill my brother. I was angry and no one could say anything to change the way I felt. I couldn't bear the thought of knowing that one of my brothers had been murdered; it just seemed impossible for it to have happened. But the reality was, it had.

I think my mother's experience with Bernard's death had to be the worst because she was the one who had to go view his body while he was still in the car at the site of where he was murdered. My brother's girlfriend's sister came to pick up Mama so that she could identify Bernard's body. On the way to identify the body, the woman driving my mother stopped at Taco Bell to get something to eat. My mother was on fire because she had to wait to identify her dead son because this girl had a craving for Taco Bell. If it had been me, I would have slapped the shit out of her, kicked her a-- out of her own car, and gone to see my brother. It's amazing how disrespectful and rude a person can be when the ghetto gets hold of one's mind, and develops immunity towards death.

Finally, Mama got to Bernard and saw him dead in the car with blood everywhere. I couldn't have bore the sight of him, in the flesh, after he had just been murdered. My mother started screaming frantically, calling out to Bernard to come to her because she didn't believe that he was dead. She fell to the ground as though her legs were paralyzed. Her son was dead. She went up to him and touched his face, to see if it was real. She told me that he was still warm and blood was still running from his head wounds. She comforted him as though he were sleeping because she wanted him to know that she loved him. Deep down Mama wanted Bernard to know that he would always be in her heart, and that she would miss him dearly. She said she started singing to him as though he was asleep because that was the only reality she could internalize— that he was in one long sleep from which he would never awake. She wanted to believe that Bernard left this world in peace and that he didn't feel any pain as those bullets pierced through his beautiful, black skin. She wanted to believe that he was in a far better place than that in which he had lived in South Central L.A.

Benny also took it hard because he had never acknowledged that his son could fall victim to the gun; jail, yes, but never murder. He mourned for Bernard, but hid his feelings deep inside; he never expressed his feeling well in front of other people. You could tell that he hurt on the inside, but he never revealed his true feelings. It seemed like my father felt better when he mourned alone. I think he felt at one with Bernard when he mourned for him, and he didn't want to share his memories with anyone else.

Travie took it hard. He was the only brother who went to the funeral. He and Bernard had started to hang around with each other quite a bit, and they had become very close, just as Bernard and I had been before I left for college. When Travie walked up the aisle towards the casket to view Bernard's body, he fainted before he could even get there. He couldn't believe that Bernard was dead and that we would never see him again, and in that instant he became spiteful toward all those who may have had anything to do with Bernard's death, an anger that defines his demeanor to this very day. It's a pain that one bears forever

My brother Peanut was incarcerated and could only do so much from jail. He wanted vengeance just like the rest of us, but he was more susceptible to acting upon this feelings. He didn't care. He would kill if he had to and show no remorse. He mourned for Bernard just like the rest of us and couldn't wait to get out of jail to avenge his death.

I felt like a piece of my life was missing, and I couldn't do anything to bring it back. Bernard had been my best friend and he was no longer in my life. We had shared a lot of ups and downs with each other; things no one else could understand or take away from my heart. I loved Bernard and would have died for him, if I had had the chance. I would die for any one of my brothers. I love them more then life itself. If I could give my life to get one more moment with Bernard, I would. He meant that much to me. As I had a dream about Grandmother, I had one about Bernard.

I dreamed Bernard and I were at the movies together. We always went to the movies together. We were sitting down, eating nachos, and I told him that somebody had told me that he was dead. He told me that we would always be together and that whoever had said that had told me a lie. I believed him. Then I woke up to reality; he really was dead. Again, I broke down in tears. These were different tears, though; I now knew that he would always be there with me. I felt that God granted me that last moment with him, so that he could tell me that he would always be with me. From that day forth, I have always felt as if Bernard was in the room with me wherever I was. Whenever I thought of him, he would always be there for me, to hear me and comfort me in my times of need, just like he did when we lived in the motel with Mama. Warmth flooded my heart, knowing that Bernard had let me know how much he really loved me.

I began to look at life from a very different perspective. Before this moment, I had always been suicidal, even at a young age, but never again. I can remember that even as a little boy, when my life became rough, I thought about killing myself. My brother's death brought back all of these memories. I really wanted to escape from the hellhole that God had placed me in, and I had tried to end it myself. From that forth, I never tried to kill myself again.

I survived after Bernard's, but I realized the pain that I was going through because of it. I hurt so deeply in my heart for the loss of my brother's life; every breath I have taken since that day is a little shallower than when Bernard was alive. I still miss him dearly. He was not only my brother, but my friend, my companion, the one who knew the pain our life had consisted of. I began to cherish the lives of my loved ones even more. I feared for Travie's life because he was still in the 'hood, and I was worried that he might be caught in the crossfire.

PERSEVERANCE

I was born into a society that gave little hope,
A society where a lot of my kind wind up on dope.
Yet I persevered.
I was told I would never gain success,
Yet I defied the odds because I did my best,
I persevered.
When my troubles were at there best and my back was against
the wall
I stood tall.
Yes I persevered.
I tried and I tried,
Never excepting defeat and holding on to my pride,
My ambitions for success never laid to rest;
My goals set high, and my emotions full of zest.
You can't stop me, you'll never hold me back,
There's no way ill let you break my stride, I will never veer
off my tracks
You'll never stop this train.
Though you may dish out some pain and give me a little rain
But ill be dam if you cloud my sunshine.
The destiny is mine.
Your thrust of hate, won't determine my fate
I will persevere.
Head high, showing no fear
Liberation is the only light I see,
My guiding star, my destiny.
Through my long journey of poverty, which try to retain
I stay focused, full speed ahead, riding my train,
And I persevered.

CHAPTER NINETEEN

THE WORST BRINGS OUT THE BEST

Life changed and from this moment on, I choose to live from a different perspective. Now I look at my society through a new set of eyes. I look at life with what I call my "third eye," which is the eye that enables you to see through the fallacies. After Bernard's death, I began to view life in order to figure out why things were the way that they were. In the scope of life, I turned my attention toward my society and realized that it was alienated from everything else that went on in the world. I then began to look at my people and realized that fighting over the same scarce resources was getting us nowhere. I became an outsider that was able to look at my past and learn from it. I learned that my people were dying over nothing, and they didn't even realize it. To them, life was just life. They settled on coping with the conditions. I want to rearrange the conditions and destroy the cycle that many of my kind are forced to endure and repeat. I realized that I had been blinded by the ills of the 'hood, and did not see a way out, until I was given the chance to pave a new route for myself. This is what I want to do for someone else, to show them a new way of viewing life.

Growing up in the inner city of South Central Los Angeles, I didn't see the opportunities that were available for me. I was closed-minded and had fallen into the cycle of the 'hood. I didn't know that I could be anything that I desired to be because society prevented me from seeing a future for myself. My society kept my third eye blind. It kept me away from the land of opportunity; I was supposed to remain a product of my environment. I was *supposed to* end up working in a fast food restaurant, which would have led me to a life of selling drugs, just like my mother. Fast food would not have gotten me the things I wanted in life. I wanted to drive a nice car and have nice clothes, but I couldn't get those things working at a fast food restaurant. I would have given in to "the norm" and started selling crack to hustle the money I needed in order to buy the things that I wanted. I believe that a large majority of my society, blinded by the ills of the 'hood, only see the poverty, gangs, and drugs that surrounded them. A large majority of youths are not able to see the light that could guide them to the land of opportunity because it is so far from their reality. Living in the 'hood is like living in a different world. You become what you see every day; that's how the cycle continues to grow. We are citizens of a morally different society. We see what is in front of us, and are unaware that there is a world beyond the one in which we live.

At one point in my life, I had also fallen into the trap of the 'hood, and it took a while before I was able to break free from the "norm" and begin moving toward a new destination. The cycle consumed my thoughts and beliefs of what life should be like for me. It controlled my emotions and feelings about the people around me and about my purpose for being placed here on this earth. I no longer possessed the untainted mind that was given to me at birth. I had been molded by my experiences and the reality of my poverty. As long as that mentality controlled my thoughts, I had no control of my life and I was bound to become a product of the system.

My third eye was blind, and I didn't regain my sight until someone gave me the opportunity to. I needed someone to direct me toward the light, so that I could see a destiny that was designed for me beyond the 'hood. I needed to grasp the understanding that I controlled my own fate; that I had a purpose in life beyond how I was living. I needed to feel like I was in control of how my life would turn out, and this is what millions of inner-city youth are denied. They are denied this light or the vision to see beyond what is in front of their eyes. They don't see past the poverty, so they accept living in it because that was their parents' reality as well as the generations that came before them.

The devastation that inner-city youth experience is overwhelming, and yet they constantly hear from others outside the community that they have been given every opportunity to succeed. They are presented with the idea that all they have to do is go to school and then they'll succeed, but that's not reality. Poverty, drugs and gangs are their reality. They have to fight harder than anyone else for the right to have a chance at tomorrow. That's their reality. They are faced with schools that don't have all of the essential materials needed to give them a proper education. At some schools I went to, we weren't even allowed to come to school early for extra help because of security reasons. Picture not being able to follow the lesson plan because pages were missing or vandalized from your book, or not being able to get extra help, or not knowing anyone that graduated high school. Wouldn't you feel like giving up, too? I did. These inequalities are only heightened in test scores that determine our eligibility to be accepted into college. Sure, I found a way out, but I was one of the lucky ones. I was able to escape the madness that had been driving me crazy for eighteen years of my life. My chance to escape began with meeting John

Douglas. I finally had the opportunity to see what others, outside the ghetto, had been talking about.

With the completion of my first semester in college, I had learned a lot about how society worked and about myself. I could see a different side of life. It excited me to know that I had a world of opportunity out there waiting for me. I escaped, but my brother didn't. Bernard's death made me realize why God gave me the opportunity to make it out of the 'hood. His death brought forth a new way of thinking for me that altered my goals in life. I now believed that I was given the opportunity to go to college, so that I could share what I have learned with the youth of the inner city. I was granted the gift of a better life so that I could show these kids that there is a way to succeed outside of the 'hood. As my college years continued, my ambition to change the ways of the 'hood grew stronger.

Travie was still in high school and was still enduring the obstacles of the 'hood. I made sure that he knew that if he wanted, he had a place to escape and stay in Washington. My greatest fear was losing another one of my brothers to the violence of the ghetto. My brother came to visit me and train for his football season one summer. It served as an outlet to get away from his problems at home. He even brought his best friend, so that they could both experience the pleasures of living in a society where they didn't have to watch their backs every time they walked down the street. Them staying with me, made me feel more at ease because I knew that my brother wasn't getting into trouble in the streets of Los Angeles. I could finally rest knowing that he was with me. My parents even thought it was a good idea. They couldn't bear the thought of losing another son.

After Bernard's murder, my parents began to clean up their

drug habit and started to cherish the time we all had together on this precious earth. They began doing little things like sending me small care packages to help me out while I was in college. They only did it a few times, but it was more than I had ever expected. I understood that they didn't have a lot of money, so I didn't expect anything from them. It truly is the thought put behind something that counts. They began calling me more often to see how I was doing. They could no longer bear the idea of my brothers and me not liking or respecting them. They became more family-oriented, which was a great thing to see and experience.

My parents really wanted us to forgive them for what they put us through, and hoped that we would understand that they were in a sick state of mind. Unfortunately, my older brother Peanut still blames them for all of his misfortunes. He can't let go of our past. For this reason, he still resents our parents. He doesn't look at them as parental figures, but as ex-crack addicts. He even uses profanity in their presence because he feels that they haven't earned the right to receive the respect typically due to parents. Even though my mother and father are heartbroken over his attitude, they now realize that there is nothing they can do to win back his respect except to continue to show how much they love him, my little brother, and me.

Travie, on the other hand, is happy to see them on their feet and off of drugs. He always encourages them to keep up the good work, and to fight through the temptations their habit presents. He knows that throughout our life, there have been times when our parents were off of drugs, but as soon as the troubles of life started piling up, the drugs returned. We always knew that when they finally decided to stop using drugs, it was only a matter of time before they would start again ... but this time feels different. They seem to have really stopped using and have no intention of using them again!

I was in Washington when their transformations were taking place, so what they did didn't affect me in the same way. It was good to hear that they were off drugs and doing well, but I felt so liberated at school, that I didn't really absorb how great of an accomplishment that was.

I became goal-oriented, and I was determined that I was never going back to the ghetto to live off my parents. I thank God that they finally became determined enough in their hearts to leave the ghetto's most dangerous pitfall behind. They finally turned their backs on drugs and became better people in the process. For the first time, they were parents whom I respected. I believe that if they can do it, anyone can. This only helps to reinforce how hard I had to work with the opportunity that I had been given to get to where I am today. This fuels my desire to help others get to where I am. I am destined, of course, to run into obstacles, but nothing is worse than the hopelessness of the ghetto ... nothing.

STILL STANDING

I was born broke, and taught that there was no hope
Yet I rose from that deadly sleep some would call a nightmare
I was taught to except what society gave me
Yet I refused, with my head high, calm voice, uttering, it won't be
me
They said that this is where I belong
I smiled, and insisted they were wrong.
Still standing.
The inequalities of my society caused my family to die
I cried, yet didn't loose my pride.
Still standing.
My education was poor
Designed to keep me locked behind that door.
So that my mind wouldn't explore.
Still standing.
I shattered the cycle that was designed for me
I rose above the odds, I broke free
Still standing
I challenged the unchallenged that exist today
I refused to settle, I searched for a better way
Still standing
They try to break me, hoping that I give up
But I refuse to close my mind, my jaws refuse to stay shut
My head high, pride strong and still standing
Though many of my kind is blinded by the confinement
We must not be content
Yet together as a nation
We most eradicate this so-called plantation.
Still standing.
And when we mold, may our people once again become whole
Fighting to break the cycle, so that we regain control
With our shoulders straight, heads high, and still standing.

CHAPTER TWENTY

A NEW VISION

I strongly believe that the mind can control your perceptions. It controls whether you have a pessimistic or an optimistic attitude. It controls how you take on adversities; whether you let them hold you down or use them as a stepping-stone. Your mind dictates how you view life and whether you feel like you're in control or whether you feel as if life is controlling you. I control my mind. It's up to me if I let people get to me or not; it's up to me to give up or keep moving ahead; and it was up to me to determine to continue my education.

Growing up, I never knew how powerful my mind could be. If I had, I would have been a lot further along than I was. I never knew that the mind could control how you reacted to negative situations on a day-to-day basis. Growing up, I just took what life had to offer at face value, nothing more. I decided I should get a master's degree, and then I took it a step further and began work on a Ph.D.; laying the foundation that would allow me to become a motivator for those who are stuck in a mindset that keeps them trapped in their own prison. My mind tells me that I have a responsibility to tell those who don't know that they can do anything that they put their mind to, that they can. I want to get them started on the right track toward success. It is my responsibility to let these kids know how much power they really possess.

The resources provided to me in the inner city of Los Angeles were quite different from the ones I had at the university. In L.A., I didn't have the tools needed to obtain a well rounded education, nor did I have the foundation needed to succeed at home. The only thing that kept me going throughout this time was the ability to see something other than the neighborhood I lived in and the people that helped me along the way. I was able to get out of my environment and experience a different way of life. This helped raise my expectations of myself to something other than gangbanging or working at a local fast food place. I was able to see corporate America for what it was. It was easy once you had the chance to figure it out. My dreams had an opportunity to grow, because my mind had an opportunity to follow them, but others aren't as lucky. These kids are unable to see the bigger picture and remain trapped within the prison of their own experiences. The inner city kids with whom I grew up with, didn't have an opportunity to see things as I did or the options, like I had with football. They didn't have a chance to get a free education or enter into an institution where they had unlimited resources.

Society didn't teach them to expand their dreams, minds, or aspirations. The dreams that did exist seemed unattainable. I heard that an education would lead to a better standard of life, but the lure of instant gratification prevented me from putting in the effort to get there. I wanted to be rich in life, but I didn't know how to get there. I had dreams and aspirations just like everyone else, but they seemed so far-fetched and out of my reach, that I learned to settle for what was in front of me.

Mainstream society was wrong when it said that I had an equal opportunity to succeed. I felt blessed to have the opportunity to work at a real estate company and be able to adjust my life goals to something beyond the 'hood. I was blessed to have athletic ability and to be able to earn a scholarship to a major university, but most people in my predicament didn't have those same opportunities. They were locked away from the chance to expand their abilities, because they felt trapped in the 'hood with no way out. Their community tells them that they have to make due with the resources they have. Yet, if they could just see beyond their immediate surroundings, their ambitions could take flight.

I can say that the 'hood reminds me of Niagara Falls. The ghetto is a society located directly under the waterfall, constantly being beaten by the unforgiving black rain of life. While living in the 'hood, you are faced with endless problems and limited solutions. When you think you have found a way out of a rough situation, the problems keep pouring down from above. It's different from real rain, because rain is seasonal, and every so often you get a break from it. A waterfall, on the other hand, is constant and you never seem to be able to catch your breath. You can breathe just enough to stay alive, but you slowly begin to drown. Eventually your breath will run out or your heart will give up.

As a society, we have allowed our morals to deteriorate to the point that we participate in acts of senseless violence, jealousy, murder, and drugs. These unacceptable behaviors have spread like weeds creating a forest of hate, envy, and death. Mainstream society constantly glorifies mortality and sugar coats the fatal flaws of the African-American community, thus creating an unrealistic picture of life in the 'hood. Although some doses of reality slip between the cracks and force mainstream society to take notice of the violence, we as a society would rather put a bandage on the problem than treat the wound. We are always looking for a quick-fix solution, rather than treating the actual problem, thus dooming ourselves to an endless cycle of poverty, drugs and violence.

The typical lifestyle of a young man growing up in my neighborhood consists of drugs, gangs, and the prison system at some level. Of course, we all have the opportunity to choose which avenues we take on any given day, but it is up to us to choose the right path. Unfortunately, it's easier to get sucked into the norms of survival, than it is to adapt to starvation for a long-term payoff. I was almost sucked into what seemed like the easier choice, until opportunity came knocking. Then the traps of my environment became more and more simple to see: either you go to school and starve because your parents can't provide for you, or you follow your instincts and get caught up in selling dope. The trap is that you are born into this lifestyle that forces you to make a choice between bad and worse. You don't get the opportunity to see beyond your environment, and you suffer for that for a lifetime. How hypocritical is it to say that everyone is born equal? I wasn't.

Struggling still exists in the 'hood, and I am a prime example of it. I almost fell for the fallacy that I couldn't make it, but fortunately I was and I will. That environment offers a limited number of chances to escape. To whom do we blame? Is it the child's fault that he was born into a society where most of his kind falls into a cycle of drugs and gangs? Are they to blame if they get caught-up in the norms of a violent community? Are they to blame when they are shut out from the rest of the world and its opportunities, or are born into poverty? *[WHO OR WHAT IS TO BLAME?]*

The friends with whom I grew up with adopted this way of life as acceptable; they saw no other way out. They began to accept the inequalities and believed that they had to make do with what was in front of them. Several of my friends started selling dope or have joined a gang. A few of them wound up dead, and several of them ended up incarcerated. They were caught-up in a cycle designed for them to look at life one way, a---backwards.

As long as inner-city kids are shutout from seeing and experiencing a new way of life, they will continue to settle for what their society gives them. They will continue to remain trapped in the 'hood without realizing there is a world of opportunity waiting for them just outside their city limits. Until more opportunity is given to kids in the inner-city communities, they will remain in poverty. There must be a bridge that leads to a more opportunistic future. If they choose to cross that bridge, there must be someone there to help them understand what's on the other side, so that they don't feel lost in a society that they don't understand. Let's give them positive choices rather than limit them to negative ones. This is where I step in.

I want to be the one who shows these kids how to live in a society that differs from the one that they know. I want to show them how to be better in society for generations to come. I want to be the bridge builder for the inner city.

What people fail to realize is that in order to expand the minds of kids in the inner city, we must introduce an avenue of hope. To be able to introduce an avenue of hope, we must remove them from their element. While doing so, the responsibility of a leader is to help them understand that it is not hard to live a successful life. I want to instill in their minds a higher set of goals and aspirations, so that they can abandon the belief that they are trapped in a society that offers no legal way to live prosperously.

My job will be to direct them towards the light that was shown to me. I will help them walk down the path of success and moral growth. I will be their training-wheels so that they can ride down the path of righteousness.

I believe that if you just tell young men and women that they can make it with an education without showing them how to use it and its long-term benefits, they will take what you say and override it with their own realities. They will continue to live for short-term goals that will satisfy their needs at that moment. To overpower their overwhelming addiction to instant gratification, they must know that someone sincerely cares about their well-being. They have to understand how to walk down a path of hope, before they can strive for it. Too many leaders have adopted quick fix solutions for the inner city. This problem took years to sink to its current level, so why wouldn't we think it would take years to fix?

Ghetto children have to understand the purpose and benefits of an education, and the empowerment that can bring. There must be an understanding of what an education will eventually do for them. There must be someone there to show them how to make their short-term goals roll into their long-term ones.

Without an education, they resort to getting what they need in a negative way. Drugs exist in their backyard, and there is an endless supply waiting for them. They see this as the fastest way to get what they want and start dealing. They are ignorant to the repercussions of selling crack because they focus on the short-term cash. They don't fully understand the effect it has on the community, or how it is destroying the essence of our culture. Their focus is trying to survive in a society that offers little hope, and they think that adapting to their environment is the best way to survive. They, like the people they despise, take advantage of the disadvantaged.

I will build a community center called "A Place of Hope," in the heart of the 'hood, so that young boys and girls have a safe haven in which to study, to hang out, and to grow as people. Inside this community center, there will be a quiet place where students can focus on their homework. There will also be a place where students can be tutored if they don't understand how to do an assignment. The center will be full of educational materials, such as paper, pencils, computers, books, disks, and so on. This will give them the resources they need to complete their assignments. The goal of the community center will be to give students an opportunity to gain both knowledge and understanding about the importance of their education. Its primary purpose will be to help children succeed, while at the same time teaching them to respect themselves. I want the center to bring opportunity to the inner city and its children, and to insure their safety. There will even be a van that will take kids home at the end of the day if they don't have another means of transportation, so that they won't have to walk home by themselves at night. I've lived in the 'hood, and I know what it's like. A land of opportunity awaits these children; we just have to guide them there.

Kids in inner-city communities need to see and experience things outside of their environment so that they can expand their perceptions of the world. The community center that I have in mind will help them to do just that. I believe that it will take a person who is totally devoted to seeing these kids succeed for the center to accomplish all of its goals. I am willing to be that person. The center will provide a basic motivational foundation for these kids. Even if it takes me my entire life, I will make sure that these kids have a place where they can dare to expand their horizons and to dream bigger dreams.

I, as a leader, must devote my time to helping these kids understand that they can make something of themselves in life. To do so, I have to show them how to make their education work for them, instead of them thinking that they are only working for their education. I will teach them that their minds are their temples of hope. In order to feel better about themselves, they have to take control of their mind's ability to remove the negative things from their lives, and make them positive! For example, if someone tells them that they are nothing and that they will never make it in this world, it is ultimately up to them whether that negativity destroys them or makes them stronger.

When their minds' get to the point that they can flip these comments and make them into a source of motivation, I will have done my job. When they can defy the odds because of the strength of their minds and a tenacious drive, they will never fail. This strength will enable them to get up and go to school and will guide them to success. Their intellect will prepare them to take the necessary steps to having a productive future. They will control the very outcome of their lives! This will be my gift as a leader and community center director. I will help them develop their minds, so that they will understand their ability to control what they desire to be. Just because they are born in an environment that is designed for them to fail, doesn't mean they have to be act like puppets for someone else to control.

I will become a mentor for those who need it and be an avenue of hope for those who don't have any other options. My plan is to build a mentor program for kids that are growing up in the inner city, so that they can get off to a good start toward their own personal success in life. The program will be volunteer-based. Volunteers will be recruited from local schools and universities so that these students can begin to understand that their teachers are there to make sure they grow morally and mentally successful.

The volunteer mentor program will provide one-on-one

guidance for the students who need it the most. Teachers who volunteer will be willing to devote their own time to giving these kids an extra hand in success, while changing the face of tomorrow. And I think they want to help; they just need a safe environment in which to do it. Students can sense when a teacher doesn't care about them or their future, and this only feeds into their negative perceptions about education. We then are faced with the challenge of changing that perception.

As a mentor, each volunteer will be responsible for letting each student know that s/he is there to help the students understand the purpose of education, its importance in their lives, and their importance as individuals. They will ultimately be responsible for guiding students down a path of success, so that they can learn to create their own path. I will be responsible for making sure that my mentors have the necessary tools that they need to effectively communicate with their students. Once established, this program will grow into a path to a peer-to-peer mentor program as well

This program will consist of students who have already been through the teacher-student program and have proven successful in their choices. It will be upper-classmen, primarily juniors and seniors, who felt like they benefited from participating in the program. I will match mentors and "mentorees" by gender, race, age, sex and hobbies.

The juniors and seniors will mentor freshman and sophomore students within their high school. It is my hope that they will help them have a smoother transition from middle school to high school. This program will be strictly voluntary; students will not be forced to do anything they do not want to do. My job will be to help them understand the importance of the mentor program, and the effect one person can have on another's life.

Mentoring will help create the bridge that is necessary for new students to make a seamless and successful transition. Hopefully, having someone who truly cares about them and their decisions will show them that there is hope.

The primary ingredient in decreasing the amount of failure among inner-city kids is to help them realize the importance of their education. To do so we must devote our most precious gifts - our time and our attention. By seeing the amount of time you are willing to devote to them, it creates a drive for success within the student and increases his/her motivation. I want to make sure that the mentors, and the students, are getting the maximum amount of benefit from this program. I want to be responsible for helping to create awareness within the community, and by doing so, helping to keep the bridge between the inner-city society and mainstream society open.

My purpose in life is to reduce the number of kids who get sucked up by poverty and the cycle that exists in the ghetto. I will reduce the number of kids who look to drugs for answers. I will reduce the number of kids who overwhelm our penitentiaries because they can't find another means to survive. I will reduce the number of inner-city kids who see no other future than the one that society has mapped out for them. I will open the third eye to the ghetto. I will help my inner-city youths make their short-term goals be the root of their long-term ones. I will be the outlet for the kids who can't seem to find one; I will encourage them to use me as a tool for a better life. I will make them aware that there is a life other than the one that they were born into. It is my duty to help them understand that they control their destiny, and the only way anyone else could, is if they give them that power to. I will teach them the power of the mind, and how to overcome their obstacles.

Anything is possible. If you are given the opportunity to make what you desire to come true, take it! Education is the key to the universe, and it's power can never be taken away from you. The mind grows just as much as you allow it to. Once you open your mind, you gain complete control over how you interpret the world. Ultimately, you are free (meaning that you are at peace within yourself and free of the exterior factors that may try to cage your ambitions and dreams). To gain complete control of your mind is to gain complete control of peace.

God has guided me through a life filled with negativity and insurmountable obstacles. He has given me the strength to overcome them, so that I may share what I have learned with those who are still trapped. This is my purpose; to bring morality into the lives of the children who deserve more than what they are being given.

Our children are our most precious gifts. For society to sit back and let thousands of innocent kids die fighting over scarce resources should be painful for anyone to watch. I will devote my life to making sure that as many kids as possible escape from that lifestyle. I will not only help them escape, but will give them the desire to help those who are still suffering once they make it out. These kids need to be cherished instead of being seen as expendable. My goal is to create awareness, so that opportunities that may have overlooked them in the past, won't make that mistake twice. Our inner-city children need an outlet, and I want to help the voice of the forgotten children of the ghetto be heard.

I will be the driving force behind our inner-city children. I refuse to sit in an office all day, secluded from the lives of the students. I will not get caught up in the hypocrisy of leadership. The students are my motivation! I'll fight for all children, despite their color, sex, race or creed. I want to work with those who want to end what has become of the ghetto community, with those who *see* through the hidden fallacies that exist in society today, and with those who want to end this cycle that our youths are going through. I want to work with people who believe that there can be change in what exists today. I want to work with people who believe that education and awareness are the keys to a successful society. Work with me, if you believe that society has an infinite amount of opportunity for all its children: black, white, Mexican, Asian and any other ethnicity of which this country is comprised.

I strongly believe that our youth are suffering from the neglect of a country. I believe that without them, there will be no future for America. Every man discovers this over time, but our youth are dying before they become men or women. We must understand the sacredness of life, and how precious and important the lives of our children are. We must instill the value of human life into the minds of our youth. The best way that we can do that is to collectively put our ideas together and come up with the best possible solution.

A good leader is a facilitator, not a dictator. I don't believe that one man or woman has the ultimate answer to the problems that exist in our educational system. Our society is made up of different people with different perspectives, and our solutions should reflect that. We have to collaborate, so that we can become stronger. I will do my part, and I ask that you do yours.

Kids are the primary purpose of my existence here and making their lives better is my ultimate reward. My ambitions only continue to grow for them and for my family. They are the two most important reasons for which I live. I create my own happiness within myself; no puppeteer controls my emotions or feelings. I firmly believe in change, and in order to change what exists today, we have to build towards a better tomorrow.

I believe that communities such as inner cities are in desperate need of active leaders who care about the future of our youth. There have been leaders throughout time, big and small, who have moved their corner of the world, now we must move ours. We will not and cannot be silenced. If we fail to create an awareness of what is going on in our urban societies, our children will continue to be forgotten.

Some people choose to be blind to the fact that they are living in a society where people are being denied an equal opportunity for success. We need people who are willing to sacrifice their fears for the lives of our youth. I believe that I can create an opportunity where one did not exist before. I believe that I can help a young man or woman see that he or she is someone special, and therefore deserves everything that life has to offer. I believe that I have the power to change the life of a child who is both physically battered and beaten by the ills of society. I believe you have that power, too. To be successful, we have to help the children believe in themselves. Without believing in themselves, no one can help them.

Our youth are suffering from the neglect of us as adults. If we want to reduce crime, disease, and poverty, we must help to build an awareness of what an impact our neglect has on our youth. They need to know that we truly care about them as people! Kids need to know that there are adults willing to listen to their problems without passing judgment. Instead of dictating to them what to do all the time, they will begin to respect and ask our opinions.

Listening to the youth of today only helps us as leaders to guide them to a greater tomorrow. We have to understand what they are facing before we can make inferences about how they should live their lives and can help them to achieve their goals. Understanding is part of building the bridge that leads to greater achievements. When a child knows that you are truly listening to what he has to say, he gains respect for you and will value your opinion because he feels as though you understand him. On the contrary, if you are not willing to listen to the information that a child is trying to share with you, you have no power and no basis to make decisions regarding his or her life because you have no idea what s/he is going through. As a leader, the most important thing you can do is to listen to the ones you are trying to lead.

Students are tired of being told that they need to do things a certain way, without taking into consideration what they are facing everyday, inside and outside of school. Kids want to feel like they can give their input on decisions being made about their lives, but ultimately they need to feel like they can trust the person making those decisions. Students who actively have a voice are more willing to work hard towards the ultimate goal. They are willing to fight to complete their goals because they feel like they had some say in setting them. Actively getting involved in the community is one of the most important forms of listening; only then can you begin to understand the situations your students are facing on a daily basis.

Not only does your involvement show the students that you care about what they are going through outside of school, but it also helps you understand the community in which you are working in. Though you may not understand everything that the students face, at least you understand some of the things that they are trying to deal with. An active leader is a successful one. I plan to be an active principal, one who seeks an understanding of his students so that he can help close the gap between success and failure. I will look for ways that I can guide my students through the obstacles that they are likely to face. I will also help them to avoid common pitfalls. Being a successful principal requires an investment of time and dedication to your students. In order for me to be useful, I have to posses these qualities. I have to possess the drive to make inner-city students' lives better and possess the tenacity to see my ambitions follow through. Fortunately for them, and me, I do.

While growing up, I experienced a great number of trials and tribulations, most of which would have destroyed the ambition of most kids, but I was stubborn! I don't believe any kid should have to go through the things that I went through as a child. Their lives can be made easier if people like you dedicate a little time to making sure that inner-city residents suffer less than they did the day before. I understand the pain that they are going through, because I have been there myself.

I know what it feels like to have your friends laugh at you because you have nothing. I have experienced the peer pressure of selling drugs or the temptation of joining a gang. I have even served my time in jail. I have seen many of my friends wind up six feet deep because they became victims of the gun. I know what it feels like to suffer because at one point that was all I knew.

I don't believe that it has to be that way. I believe my experience will help me be an outlet for many innocent kids who don't deserve to be in the predicaments into which they were born. I believe that our youth is suffering. The only way I can dilute some of it is by showing them that there is an end to their miserable condition. I believe I can help pave the route that they were denied and be an example of someone who truly found a way to succeed. I can give them hope where there is none.

Our youths are like sponges, they suck up everything that happens to them and around them. All it takes is a little time and effort to make sure that they have a chance. What the inner-city kids need is someone who is willing to give them their time and guidance. Someone who can paint a perfect picture of opportunity and at the same time guide them down the path until they are able to walk on their own. I truly believe that I can motivate these kids to reach for the stars. I believe that what they need is someone who believes in them, so that they can start believing in themselves. I will bring hope into their hearts and strength into their minds and, ultimately, end their suffering and stop the black rain.

LAST WORD

Here we have embarked upon the last chapter of my book, and I only can pray that you understand the purpose of my memoir. There are millions of young innocent children going through the same heartache that I had once endured as an adolescent growing up in the inner city. We will never fully understand the training that occurs in these young kids lives because we cant, nor do we wish to walk in their shoes. They face violence in their homes, on the streets in which they walk, in their schools and even in the music that the media allows on television. Coupled with 360-degrees of negativity, their primary choices all lead to temptations that their environment offers, i.e., drugs, gangs, violence, prison and death. Yet they are judged by a fate that they could not control. The misleading illusions tell them that the only choices they face all exist in the "hood." Being that I am still headed toward my purpose in life, I can now continue to fulfill my heart's hunger for a better life for these kids. I now work in an inner-city school in Chicago, where I am one of the assistant principals in my school. I can now further my dream, my desire, my ambition, and most of all, my true purpose of working towards opening my own school. I want to continue to move towards improving the lives of thousands of innocent kids'. Let the truth be told, I could not dream of a better job or way to live my life. The opportunity given to me from the spirit up above has opened my eyes to endless possibilities in improving the lives of these kids. Fantasy is what people want, but reality is what they need and is what will set them free.

The majority of our youth roam the streets absent of a direction. My purpose and my goal for this book is to let the misdirected youth understand that opportunity exists. Even though the light is dim, it still exists. I am here to guide inner-city youths to that light, with hopes that they follow the path that will lead them to an avenue of choices. Our kids *have been neglected for far too long.*

It is now time for you, the youth, to begin to understand the power of education. Look at what lurks in your neighborhoods today, drugs, violence, prisons, liquor stores, and endless poverty. You are designed to embrace what you see. You are programmed to believe that all that exists in this world is in your small neighborhood, and that anything else does not fit your lifestyle. It's all lies; the world is yours. Go out and embark on new journeys, so that your minds, dreams, ambitions, and opportunities will grow. Refuse to settle for what was given to you at birth. Don't just give up on life because you see others around you do it. Create your own path so that you control your destiny. Don't be a puppet and let others control your future, your emotions and your dreams.

It took my mother and my father a long time to realize that the only person who can control their future is the one person they have to look at in the mirror everyday. Once they figured that out, they began to change their lives. It took them that long to realize that if their son can do it, then so can they. My mother is now off of drugs and in college working on her AA degree, and my father is doing the same. Even though they are not together as a couple, they are still heading in the right direction, which makes me proud to call them my parents. I forgive them for the heartache and the pain that they put my brothers and me through, because I now realize what they went through growing up in the 1960s. They, too, were brainwashed into believing that their environment was all that they had to embrace in life. Both of them did not graduate from high school, so they were guided by ignorance and the manifested knowledge that the "hood" offered them. I can now not only visualize their struggle, yet in some ways I can empathize with their pain.

In closing, I pledged to dedicate my life to educating the inner city youth on the importance of opening their minds and embracing education and a life other than the one they have to endure in their neighbor-

hoods. *I will try my best to develop educational programs that help inner-city youth experience life outside of their neighborhoods, so that they have hands-on experience in understanding that they can function outside of their immediate environment. I will help develop resources to provide financial support for the thousands and thousands of inner-city kids who lack the resources to effectively attend college. And finally, I will dedicate my life to helping the youth grow up to be better people. I plan on achieving this goal of mine by leading by example. Despite all of the educational achievements or financial stability a person possesses, if they do not know how to be good people, all of their monetary possessions become inconsequential. There are too many innocent kids dying day by day who need the help of good people, and if I can't teach others how to help, then I must ask myself what is my true purpose here on earth.*

BIRDS OF A FEATHER
FLOCK TOGETHER

A place of birth, where my soul is cursed, along with a precon-
ceived destiny, which is lying face up in a hearse
It's a shame how I've been trained not to use my brain, in a soci-
ety consumed with pain
The black rain leaves unwanted stains in this manifestation,
which contains an overload of crack cocaine
So through this training process my life is bombarded with stress
Now I must confess, my heart is consumed with unhappiness,
because every where I go I have to pray that I don't get shot in the
chest
Do you see the bitterness, or do you choose to ignore
Come walk with me through this war and witness how many of
our young babies lie dead on the floor
We are poor and don't anyone adore our beautiful black faces, so
what are we living for
We are created out of habit, breed like rabbits, stuck in a paradox,
filled with panic
So now we run frantic for our lives, ducking and dodging bullets,
searching for places to hide
This is how we are created, and unfortunately this is why we are
hated, segregated and perpetuated as illiterate
You see, they premeditated manifested and invested in our down-
fall
It was driven by hatred, mixed in with faceless racist, who want-
ed to see us trapped in these places
Combined with no one who is considerate of our existence
So without persistence, we continue to have an empty conscience,

because we know that no one wants us

So without a fuss, we accept the crust of life and convince ourselves that's its right

This is one of the reasons why we won't unite

Because despite all of the hidden opportunities, we cant even contemplate the idea of unity

We are too busy focused on the now, that the later refuses to consume our thoughts

It's because we bought into the created thought

Well if you didn't catch the lesson, it is now about to be reiterated

They premeditated, manifested and invested in our downfall

It was driven by hatred, mixed in with faceless racist, who wanted to see us trapped in unhappiness

Along with a psychological plantation, caging us from our destination, with this ongoing infiltration

I said with this ongoing infiltration we are consumed with anger and frustration, so please embrace this education, because it will soon spark your imagination

For right now, our minds is in retention, not to mention the severity of our prosperity

Now I hope I have delivered this message with clarity because rarely do I get a chance to open the minds of others

Others meaning my sisters and brothers

So in ending the word, I hope you set your mind free because for far too long its been caged like a bird

Don't give up the fight, because we will unite and go on believing that tomorrow will be bright

Just don't give in because our world is consumed with sin, because as long as I'm breathing, you'll always have a friend

For more information about our author or
to order this book please contact:

In Time Publishing & Media Group
75 East Wacker Dr., 10th Floor
Chicago, Illinois 60601
Tel: (312) 419-9100
Fax: (312) 419-9400
www.intimepublishing.com